Norfolk & Western Railway's Magnificent Mallets
The Y Class 2-8-8-2s

By

William E. Warden

TLC PUBLISHING

1993
TLC Publishing, Inc.
Route 4 - Box 154
Lynchburg, Virginia 24503-9711

Front Cover Illustration: Voluminous exhaust dwarfs husky Y-6 No. 2130 as she digs in at Lowry, near Bedford, Virginia, about 1954, with a train of empty hoppers. The summit of Blue Ridge is 22 miles away but already the grade is working against the 2130, and you can be certain there'll be a continuous pyrotechnic display such as this until the summit is crested. *[This painting commissioned especially for this book is by Andrew Harmantas.]*

Dedication

This book is dedicated to the memory of H. Reid (1925-1992). For over 35 years, H. was my friend, mentor, and confidant; my brother, my other self. His sudden death left a void in my life and in the lives of so many other people, including his wife Ginny, who knew and loved this internationally-known rail writer and photographer (some of his photos grace the pages of this book). H., wherever you are today, I hope there is a never-ending procession of heavenly Y-6s slogging up some celestial Christiansburg Hill or Blue Ridge grade. God be with you H. Reid, in your journey through eternity.

Bill Warden

First Printing, 1993
Second Printing, 1996

Library of Congress Catalog Number 93-60179
International Standard Book Number 1-883089-01-8

Typography & Layout by
Thomas W. and Carolyn B. Dixon

Printed by
Walsworth Publishing Co.
Marceline, MO

Contents

Acknowledgements

Authoring this book without the generous assistance of a great many people, many of whom were far more knowledgeable than I on matters of N&W Mallets, would have been a Herculean task. As it was, the assistance was always given willingly and received gratefully. And for their help, I would like to extend humble thanks to the following who made this book a reality: William R. Baumgardner, Jr., Arthur M. Bixby, Sr., C. W. Burns, Richard J. Cook, Sr., Ed Crist, Thomas W. Dixon, Jr., George Heiron, Eugene L. Huddleston, C. W. Jernstrom, E. W. King, John Krause, Lloyd D. Lewis, Steve Patterson, H. Reid, Dennis E. Quillen, J. R. Quinn, Jeff Sanders, Joe Schmitz, Jim Shaughnessy, Robert D. Simpson, and Harold K. Vollrath.

And I would like to extend a special thank you to all those Norfolk & Western company photographers. These men, most of whom were not railfans, worked in relative obscurity to produce silver images that were technically perfect and not infrequently examples of railroad art at its best.

William E. Warden
Waynesboro, Virginia
January, 1993

Jim Shaughnessy

No. 2160, a Y6a 2-8-8-2 Mallet leads a second Y doubleheaded with a coal train on Blue Ridge grade in August 1958. By then every other Class I railroad in the U. S. was dieselized or nearly so, yet N&W was still using these highly refined compound locomotives to produce some of the best operating ratios in the business. Their design is traced to 1910 when the first compound articulateds were purchased by N&W. The development of the type continued in the ensuing decades until the ultimate Mallet of the 1950s shown here. This angle accentuates the slightly above-center smokebox door on the Y-6a.

Introduction

Back in steam days, every railroad had its "workhorses." These were versatile locomotives that could handle just about any job an imaginative road foreman of engines could dream up.

Originally designed for slow "drag" service, workhorses were quite at home doing humping and yard switching. They could wander down remote branches with locals, help push 100-car coal drags up tortuous grades, or muscle work trains out on the mainline. And if circumstances demanded it, power a manifest freight or two--a chore that would sometimes require doubleheading two workhorses. This versatility frequently allowed workhorse locomotives to survive long after more glamorous steamers had been replaced by diesels.

A workhorse could be of almost any wheel arrangement. Most popular in this service in post-World War II days were 2-8-2s and 2-10-2s. Norfolk & Western Railway had its workhorses too—but the N&W was, and still is, no usual railroad.

Instead of a single 2-8-2, the N&W workhorse was the equivalent of two 2-8-2s but with a single boiler and firebox and operated by a single crew. In short, the N&W's steam workhorses were the various Y-class articulated 2-8-8-2s with the forward set of eight drivers pivoted with respect to the boiler to allow the locomotive to negotiate sharp curves. It is no coincidence that the last steam locomotive to be called for on-line service before the N&W declared itself 100-percent dieselized was a workhorse 2-8-8-2.

Not only were the Y's articulated, but they were also compound or Mallet locomotives (named for Swiss designer Anatole Mallet, who originated the concept, and whose name rhymes with "alley").

A compound locomotive used steam twice. It was first fed directly from the boiler into a pair of high-pressure cylinders. The high-pressure cylinder exhaust, instead of being shot up the exhaust stack directly, was fed to a pair of low-pressure cylinders through flexible (because of articulation) piping, and the low-pressure exhaust was then transferred to the stack. In order to keep the exhaust plumbing as uncomplicated as possible, the low pressure cylinders on a Mallet were placed up front as close to the stack as possible.

Most of the N&W's later Mallets also had a provision for "jump starting," wherein boiler steam could be fed through a reducing valve directly into the low-pressure cylinders at startup. Thus a Y could be operated "simple" at low speeds. This feature was generally cut off—at first automatically and in later years by the locomotive engineer—at around 10 mph.

Additionally, some of the last Y's were built with an arrangement for giving the low-pressure cylinders a shot of high-pressure steam directly from the boiler whenever faster acceleration or extra tractive effort was needed (see page 9). This latter feature was also added to many older Y's as they entered Roanoke Shops for overhaul.

The reusing of steam in compound locomotives squeezed every last BTU possible out of it before it was finally exhausted. Thus, all other things being equal, the thermal efficiency and maximum tractive effort of a compound Mallet locomotive were considerably greater than that of an articulated being operated "simple," that is with the boiler steam fed directly into all cylinders and none of it reused except to create a draft. As is so frequently the case, however, all other things were NOT equal and the Mallet never reached the level of efficiency envisioned by its inventor.

From the time the Baltimore & Ohio received the first Mallet built in this country, an 0-8-8-0, in 1904 until 1924 when the N&W became the sole builder of them, the term "Mallet" was almost synonymous with "Articulated." And even until the very end of the steam age, simple articulated locomotives were frequently, albeit erroneously, referred to as Mallets. Old habits do not die easily.

If Mallets truly were at least somewhat more efficient than simple articulateds, why did Alco, Baldwin, etc., suddenly stop building the compounds in the 1920s and concentrate on constructing only simple articulateds?

Speed, which railroads seem to have discovered in the 1920s, just as motor trucks were taking to the highways in significant numbers, was the primary

H. K. Vollrath

Not a heavy locomotive by any means, W-2 class 2-8-0 No. 690 had been one of N&W's principal freight haulers before the arrival of the articulateds. This 45-year-old engine was still in steam at Lynchburg, Virginia, in April 1950.

reason. Running trains faster was the only way for the rails to retain their freight business, and Mallets were inherently slow. Then too, the introduction of the feedwater heater, which used exhaust steam to heat incoming boiler water, made the efficiency of a simple articulated comparable to that of a Mallet—about 7 percent.

Why were Mallets so slow, and why did the N&W continue to build them right alongside their high-speed A-class simple articulated 2-6-6-4s? Answers to the first part of the question are easier to come by than answers to the second.

For efficient operation of any articulated locomotive at any operating speed, it is desirable that the two sets of drivers share the load—that is, the generation of tractive effort and horsepower—equally. In a simple articulated this is no problem. Both sets of drivers and cylinders are the same size, both sets of cylinders receive steam at the same pressure and the same cutoff. And if engine weight can be balanced so that there is equal weight on each driver set, the load is balanced regardless of whether the locomotive is doing 10 miles per hour or 70.

A Mallet is different. Total pressure—that is the force in pounds exerted by steam on the piston surfaces to produce tractive effort—of the low-pressure cylinders is hardly ever the same as that of the high-pressure cylinders. When a train is just starting up and maximum tractive effort is required, the engineer sets his power reverse lever "down in the corner" and boiler steam is admitted to the high-pressure cylinders for the entire (or almost the entire) piston stroke. Under this condition the steam fed to the low-pressure cylinders will be at its maximum possible pressure and the front set of drivers will be exerting their maximum tractive effort.

But as the train speeds up and less tractive effort is required, the engineer will move the power reverse back and thus reduce the "cutoff." Cutoff is the percent of the piston stroke during which steam is admitted. If cutoff were not reduced, the effect on fuel consumption and speed would be comparable to running your Chevy in low gear on a rural Interstate highway. As the cutoff is reduced, the pressure of the high-pressure cylinder exhaust is also reduced and the steam is fed to the low-pressure cylinders at ever decreasing pressure.

This decreased pressure alone will decrease the proportion of tractive effort produced by the low-pressure cylinders, and the locomotive's overall drawbar horsepower, after rising to a maximum at, say, 25 mph, will drop quite rapidly as speed is increased further.

There is, however, one other piece of mischief that exacerbates matters: back pressure on the low-pressure cylinders caused by exhausting the low-pressure steam through the nozzle and the stack. This back pressure makes it more difficult for the exhaust to exit the stack as cutoff is reduced. In turn, this produces less draft in the firebox and a corresponding tendency for boiler pressure to drop. This drop in boiler pressure will cause horsepower to drop off even more rapidly after some optimum speed is reached—around 25 mph on N&W 2-8-8-2s.

One problem associated with reduced cutoff is compensated for partially by simply enlarging the low-pressure cylinder diameter, since, all other things being equal, total pressure on the piston and hence the tractive effort it produces is directly proportional to the piston area. Note that even if boiler steam was fed directly to a high-pressure cylinder throughout a piston stroke, the pressure of steam fed to the low-pressure cylinders would be reduced somewhat by the cooling effect of the piping connecting the two cylinders. Some Mallets, particularly the Virginian Railway's 2-10-10-2s, had low-pressure cylinders big enough for a full-grown man to sit inside. However, bridge and tunnel clearances, plus the amount of available space under the boiler, limit how large a cylinder can be.

The N&W's Y's had 39-inch diameter low-pressure cylinders verses 24-1/2- or 25-inch high-pressure. Dynamometer car tests on one of the newest Y's held in the early 1950s showed peak drawbar horsepower of approximately 5,500 at 25 mph, but that as speed was increased above this, the horsepower quickly decreased. By comparison, the A-class 2-6-6-4 simple articulated tested at that time had a peak drawbar horsepower of only 5,200, but this was not reached until locomotive speed was approximately 35 mph, and it was still 5,000 at 60 mph.

The Mallet was certainly a slow locomotive, suitable only for drag and helper service, or yard work, according to conventional wisdom. Which brings us to the second part of our big question: Why did N&W continue to build Mallets side by side with its high-stepping A's? And why were the Y's built by Roanoke well into 1952, whereas Roanoke constructed the last A in 1950?

Answers are not so obvious, especially when you consider that both of the N&W's Pocahontas-region neighbors, the Chesapeake & Ohio and Virginian railways, took delivery on their last Mallets in 1923. Some of the Virginian's USA and USB class 2-8-8-2s were still in operation when the road diselized in 1955. And C&O did buy a group of 10 compound 2-6-6-2s in 1948 closing out its purchases of new steam locomotives with a design not changed from 1920 (basically used to replace older locomotives of this type in slow coal mine run work).

Was it allegiance to coal? After all in the mid-1950s the black diamonds consistently provided N&W with better than 65 percent of its freight revenue. A possible consideration but not a major one. The C&O was just as dependent on coal, yet it received no steam whatsover after 1948.

Three factors pretty much account for the phenomenon on N&W. First was the line's profile. It had more and steeper mainline grades than either of its

William E. Warden Coll.

Life before the Y's came. Young ladies sitting on a fence wave at brave crews of helper engines on Christiansburg Hill, shoving a 4-wheel caboose, a design popular around 1900. Pushing are M-class 4-8-0 No. 462 and a second unidentifable M. Date is around 1906-1910. When the X-1s and Y-1s arrived in 1910 a single locomotive replaced the tandems seen here on this grade.

Pocahontas neighbors, even in areas that were, relatively speaking, flat.

Thus, a Y was powerful enough to get heavy coal trains over the hills and dales at reasonable speeds, and with greater efficiency and tractive effort than could have been provided by any other type of locomotive. Had N&W's mainline east of Roanoke looked like that of the Virginian with the latter's maximum compensated grades of 0.2 percent eastbound and 0.6 percent westbound, possibly N&W would have opted for 2-8-4s to get the coal to Tidewater, as did the Virginian.

Second was that N&W's motive power department had been designing and building in Roanoke Shops its own locomotives as early as 1911 when the highly successful M-2a-class 4-8-0s began leaving the erecting floor. N&W corporate officials reasoned that the road had enough in-house talent to design and build Mallets that would conquer virtually all existing design problems—locomotives that could even pull heavy manifest freights with no apologies. Additionally, there was still enough drag freight territory around to justify high tractive effort at low speeds.

The third factor was one other motive power department decision, made in the 1930s. All design and building efforts were concentrated on just three types of locomotives: the J-class 4-8-4s for passenger service, A-class 2-6-6-4s for fast mainline freights plus protecting passenger schedules, and Y's for just about everything else. By comparison, neighboring C&O was buying poppet-valved 4-6-4s (the heaviest Hudson types ever built) and 4-8-4s for passenger service, 2-8-4s for fast freight east of Clifton Forge, Virginia, and occasionally passenger service, 2-6-6-2s (a design N&W had previously abandoned) for coal drags, and mammoth 2-6-6-6s to move coal across the Alleghanies between Hinton, West Virginia, and Clifton Forge, Virginia.

With only three locomotive types to consider and all of them built in house, parts could be made interchangeable with considerable cost savings plus increased manufacturing efficiency, and lessons learned from one class could easily be applied to the others.

One other reason for sticking with the Mallets bears consideration: N&W President R. H. "Race Horse" Smith, whose devotion and unabashed admiration for steam locomotives plus knowledge of job details, were legendary. Smith had gone to work for the N&W straight out of Princeton and never worked anywhere else.

Ironically, Smith presided over the beginning of N&W dieselization. A 1958 EMD advertisement featured the portrait of a dour Smith against an artist's rendering of hoppers and a Geep. Part of the ad quotes Smith as saying, "With this (Clinch Valley) District fully Dieselized, we will be able to move coal efficiently and economically." One wonders if old "Race Horse" choked on those words.

The official reasoning might have seemed brash at the time to outside observers but management was right and N&W's operating ratio continued to be one of the lowest in the industry, even when the N&W was the lone steam holdout among Class I railroads.

Out of the motive power department and off the

Roanoke erecting floor came a fleet of fat-boilered locomotives whose banshee wail of a whistle and clanking side rods could be heard for more than 37 years along every mile of the main line from Norfolk to Cincinnati and Columbus, the Lynchburg-Durham line, the Shenandoah Division from Winston-Salem to Hagerstown, down to Bristol and Norton, and onto innumerable branches in the rugged Pocahontas coal country.

These were locomotives that could and would pull 14,000 tons on the Scioto Division and take 200-car coal trains east from Blue Ridge; locomotives that could work the Portsmouth hump yard or mine runs 24 hours a day (setting aside an hour now and then to be coaled, watered, and lubed); and end up on the point of red ball freights everywhere. Even after the the coming of the A's, so-called "Potato Specials," solid trains of refrigerator cars and ventilated box car cars filled with spuds from Norfolk and Petersburg to Ohio, moved behind Y's as late as 1939. They eventually hauled everything from coal to automobiles, chemicals, grain, furniture, and cheese.

If that wasn't enough evidence of versatility, in June 1958, a Y-6 hauled five passenger coaches and two gondolas full of gawking locals on a tour of Buchanan County (Virginia) to help celebrate its centennial. And a year later, in the very twilight of steam, Y-6b No. 2174 was the co-star of a "Rail Museum Safari" Roanoke-Bluefield-Iaeger fan trip in July 1959. A-class 2-6-6-4 No. 1240 handled the Roanoke-Bluefield leg of the run, but then hauling the varnish was nothing exceptional for an A.

About the only place where 2-8-8-2s couldn't make the grade, in a manner of speaking—at least for several decades—was in the vicinity of West Virginia's Elkhorn Tunnel, where a rise of 105 feet to the mile (a 1.8 percent grade), 13-degree curves, and poor tunnel ventilation made navigating this piece of real estate hazardous to an engine crew's health. The tunnel, plus trackage between Bluefield and Vivian, was electrified in 1914. This electrification was ultimately extended to Iaeger.

A line relocation, including a new Elkhorn Tunnel with better ventilation and 1.4 percent ruling grade was opened in June 1950, allowing the catenary to be taken down, and 2-8-8-2s finally to conquer every Appalachian hill on Norfolk & Western. This was one of the few times in history that steam ever supplanted electric power on an American railroad. It was also the last time.

There was no single class of Y's as there was of the A's. Rather the Y design evolved gradually until there were 10 different sub-classes, ranging from the slim-boilered Baldwin-built Y-1, constructed in 1910, to the state-of-the-art Y-6b, the first of which left Roanoke Shops in 1948. Existing classes were frequently modified following years of service. Sometimes the changes were as minor as recessing tender backup lights on Y-4s, Y-5s, and Y-6s in 1947 to eliminate damage from water spouts, or installing outsized sand boxes on Y-5s; other times as major as adding roller bearings. Additionally, locomotives of a particular sub-class sometimes differed one from another as the motive power department continued to fine tune each design. Indeed, pre-World War I Y's had little in common with post-World War II ones except compounding and a common wheel arrangement.

Some of this fine-tuning explains why Y-4 class 2-8-8-2 No. 2083, a 1927 American Locomotive Company (Richmond Works) product, was spied spreading cinders on Blue Ridge grade on the same October 1957 day that Y-6b No. 2175, a 1948 Roanoke Shops product, was doing likewise. Only difference: the 2175 was leading another Y on an eastbound coal train while 2083 was powering a humble local. The 2083, by the way, was an old friend of the author's as it regularly used to amble into Waynesboro, Virginia, his home town, around 7:00 a.m. with a local from Shenandoah. (On a July Saturday in those days, and without stepping outside the corporate limits of Waynesboro, one could photograph the 2083, a K-2 class 4-8-2 on the point of No. 1, the "New York train," at least two other Y's on manifest freights, and Waynesboro Yard's faithful switcher, M-2 class 4-8-0 No. 1119, in action between sunup and breakfast. With all that smoke, steam, wailing whistles, ringing bells, and clanking side roads, Satuday mornings didn't come any better!)

Mallets in general—and Y's were no exception––were not handsome in the style of say, a Union Pacific Challenger, but they weren't meant to be. The late Trains editor, David P. Morgan, comparing the aestetics of A's and Y's said: "The engines were as similar as a debutante and a barmaid." A more apt choice of similes, particularly when viewing them head-on, might be "greyhound and pit bull."

The outsized low-pressure cylinders gave a Y the appearance of having congenital mumps. As with most Mallets, the pilot deck, surely big enough to carry a Volkswagen, seemed intended to separate the smokebox and the forward coupler by as much space as a turntable would allow. Then there was that miniscule trailing truck squeezed under the cab supporting a scant 27,000 pounds of a Y-4's 567,000 pounds of engine weight. One might reasonably suspect it was added by a distraught motive power department middle manager after the design went into production. Spoked wheels and inside journals on the earlier Y's trailing trucks did nothing for aestetics either.

No matter. For this author, who photographed his first Y back in 1950 and did not see an A until five years later, the Y's strength and unflagging power gave them an element of excitement and—despite their pugnacious appearance—a charm and fascination that no other Norfolk & Western locomotive ever produced.

Development of the Y-Class 2-8-8-2

How, when, and why were ten classes of a single wheel arrangement designed and built? For answers to this batch of questions, we must go back almost two decades before the first Y-class turned a wheel.

In the late 1890s and early 1900s, when the heaviest mainline rail weighed but 85 pounds to the yard, most N&W freight was hauled by F-, G-, and W-class 2-8-0s, plus 15 U-class Vauclain cross-compound 4-6-0s. These latter engines also were used in passenger service. Fine locomotives— enough so that two G's were still earning their keep as late as the mid-1950s. But their modest tractive effort (24,480 pounds for older G's—29,376 pounds for the G-1 subclass—and 40,163 pounds for the W's) limited their ability to cope with the rapid increase in train size experienced by N&W in the early 1900s. A not uncommon sight in those days was *three* 2-8-0 helpers straining to boost a train of modest proportions, 1,800 or 2,000 tons, up Christiansburg Hill.

Attempting to come up with a locomotive powerful enough to deliver freight from one side of Christiansburg Hill or Blue Ridge grade to the other, N&W began buying M-class 4-8-0s from Richmond and Baldwin Locomotive Works in 1906.

Splendid engines the 4-8-0s were. They could run like freightened deer on level track thanks to four-wheel pilot trucks and larger boilers. Later versions developed more tractive effort than Consolidation types (2-8-0s). So splendid was the design that many M's were still turning a dollar for the railroad as late as 1957. N&W ultimately owned 286 examples of this rare wheel arrangement, more than any other railroad in America.

But even the 4-8-0s couldn't keep pace with the increased tonnage—particularly coal tonnage—being handled by the railway. So in 1910, N&W received its first newfangled Mallets, five X-1-class 0-8-8-0s from ALCO and another five Y-1-class 2-8-8-2s from Baldwin.

Aside from differing in wheel arrangements, the two classes had other mechanical distinctions. Both had piston valves on the rear, high-pressure cylinders, but the X's had slide valves on their low-pressure frot cylinders, whereas the Y-1s had piston valves on theirs. Both classes however, had 56-inch drivers, carried 200 pounds boiler pressure and had provisions for reheating the high-pressure cylinder exhaust before feeding it to the low-pressure cylinders. The X-1s were numbered 990-994 and the Y-1s 995-999.

Just why Norfolk & Western opted for equal numbers of these two different wheel arrangements at the same time is not clear. A plausible theory is that Mallets with and without pilot and trailing trucks were being built and sold at that time and N&W, always a railroad to look for the finest and able to afford it too, simply wanted to find out which type would best meet its needs. The fact that dynamometer car tests were run on both types shortly after delivery supports this theory.

Intuition suggests that the tests would show the 2-8-8-2s to be the superior type. Indeed, when it came to tracking around curves Y-1s were superior: they had none of the disconcerting "yaw" (sudden, erratic deviation from course) that a locomotive without a pilot truck suffers.

But at the slow speeds of most N&W drag freight yawing was tolerable. Those 4-8-0s could still handle any freight that had to get over the road in a hurry. Tonnage was the name of the game and the X-1s proved capable of digging in with 3.6 percent more tonnage than the 2-8-8-2s and surprisingly, could haul that extra tonnage at a speed almost 20 percent faster than the Y-1s. Worse still, the Y-1s suffered almost continuously from leaky flues and other ailments.

Actually, all locomotives in those days suffered from leaks, usually from the boiler. A standard ploy of N&W engine crews was to carry a bucket of sawdust in the cab. When steam started issuing from unseemly places, the crew would dump some sawdust into the injector. The water-borne sawdust would then find and plug up the leaks until more permanent repairs could be made.

H. K. Vollrath Coll.

M-Class 4-8-0s, of which No. 457 is representative, were among the forerunners of the Y's. When bumped from mainline freight chores, the M's stayed on the roster many years powering branch-line trains and handling switching duties. The N&W accounted for two-thirds of the country's Twelve-wheelers. Photo is at Kenova, West Virginia, in October 1949.

William E. Warden Coll.

First cousin to the Y, No. 990 was one of five X-1 class 0-8-8-0s delivered to N&W by ALCO in 1910, the same year that Baldwin built five Y-1s for the line. The X-1s had superior pulling power but the lack of a pilot truck limited them to low-speed operation, and ultimately hump-yard service.

Thus the five star-crossed Y-1s were scrapped in 1924. Two of them, minus their running gear, spent some of their more productive years supplying steam to the Shaffers Crossing engine terminal. By comparison, the five 0-8-8-0s, albeit relegated ultimately to hump yard service, stayed on the roster until 1934. Drawbacks aside, both the X-1s and the Y-1s did prove that an articulated locomotive with two sets of eight drivers could move far more tonnage across Blue Ridge and Christiansburg Hill without recourse to a helper engine than anything else in the roundhouse.

World War I, with its greatly increased need for Pocahontas coal (a favorite fuel of the German Navy, incidentally) and other freight necessary for waging a war, hastened the testing of the motive power department's hypothesis that articulateds were the ultimate answer to moving tonnage. In March 1918, under the direction of A. Kearney, Superintendent of Motive Power, and Mechanical Engineer J. A. Pilcher (who was part of the team that later developed the A-class 2-6-6-4s), Roanoke Shops turned out its first home-built articulated: a brute of a 2-8-8-2 numbered 1700.

Boasting the then high boiler pressure of 230 pounds (later increased to 270 pounds), piston valves on all cylinders, a face full of air compressors to cope with the narrow bridge and tunnel clearances which prevented them being placed on the side of the boiler as was normal practice, and 56-inch drive wheels, the new Mallet was designated class Y-2. Ultimately, Roanoke built four more identical locomotives and Baldwin 20 for N&W. The Roanoke locomotives were numbered 1700-1704 and the Baldwins 1711-1730.

In an attempt to increase overall tractive force, three of the Y-2s, Nos. 1702, 1706, and 1714, were equipped in 1930 with Franklin boosters on their tenders and another two, 1700 and 1711, with Bethlehem boosters in 1931. Since the boosters only reached maximum effectiveness when the tender was full, or nearly so, and required additional piping with the attendant problems of flexible joints, this modification was not added to all locomotives. (At least one Y-3, No. 2006, was equipped with Bethlehem boosters.) In later years the booster-equipped Mallets were used primarily for switching duties in Norfolk, Roanoke, and Portsmouth.

The Y-2s were durable too. In 1951 some were still hauling "fuel satisfaction" (N&W's catch phrase at the time for coal) on the main line. Others shed their boiler-tube pilots in the late 1930s, which were replaced with ordinary footboards, and went into yard switching service. The N&W was not one to scrap perfectly good engines, even when newer ones were added to the roster.

As was the case with all wars, the First World War created its own melange of bureaucracies. One of these was the United States Railroad Administration (USRA), decreed by President Woodrow Wilson in March

H. K. Vollrath Coll.

Brand new, Y-1 No. 999 poses for its official Baldwin company photograph in 1910. Note the oil headlight perched high atop the boiler, a design that tended to leave the track in darkness when the Mallet rounded sharp curves. Later Y designs placed the headlight on the pilot beam so it would swivel with the lead set of wheels and stay focused on the track.

H. K. Vollrath Coll.

The place is Roanoke, the date is 1910 and N&W has just received Y-1, No. 999, an occasion for these diverse gents in bowler hats, vests and watch fobs, probably N&W functionaries—a yardmaster, a road foreman, maybe even a vice-president—to be photographed with their new behemoth.

1917. Among the USRA's first acts was to nationalize the nation's rail lines, an act which the railroads, with a rare burst of unanimity, condemned.

But even a blind hog can stumble on an acorn. The USRA's acorn was establishing a committee of rail and locomotive builder executives who then agreed upon the best possible standardized designs for a dozen different types of steam locomotives with largely interchangeable parts, deemed necessary for the war effort, and which could be used interchangeably on all American railroads. The USRA 2-8-8-2 design happily was based on N&W's Y-2-class. (The Y-2s were slightly lighter but had greater tractive effort than the final USRA design).

Over 2,000 USRA locomotives of all types were eventually built, many long after peace had returned. Locomotives sired by Roanoke's ingenuity were still pounding the nation's rails when another world war started and for many years thereafter. The N&W Motive Power Department had ample cause for being proud.

Although the Y-2 was the prototype for the USRA heavy compounds, the government agency placed no restrictions on what Roanoke could build; these restrictions applied only to Baldwin, Lima, and ALCO, and such ALCO affiliates as the Richmond Locomotive Works. Thus Roanoke, with six Y-2 boilers that didn't quite meet USRA specifications, was able to perform its first experiment in fine-tuning locomotive design. The result was creation of the Y-2a class 2-8-8-2 in 1924. Actually, the Y-2a's differed only superficially from the Y-2s. The Y-2a's were numbered 1705-1710, had 57-inch drivers and high-pressure cylinder diameter was increased from 24-1/2 to 25 inches.

Both classes survived into the late 1940s and an earnest but untutored railfan in, say 1925, would have needed a micrometer and calipers to distinguish one from the other in appearance. Eventually the Y-2a's were equipped with 18,000-gallon, 26-ton tenders which made differentiating them from the Y-2s easier since the latter had 12,000-gallon, 20-ton tenders. A 1945 Motive Power Department Y-2a drawing shows the smokebox without air pumps, but the number of engines so modified is not known.

Interestingly enough, while the railway was tinkering with the Y-2 design, it received from Baldwin and ALCO 50 USRA-design 2-8-8-2s in 1919 and labeled them Y-3 class. Thus we have the odd situation of all Y-2a's actually being built five years after the Y-3s. With the introduction of the Y-3s, N&W Mallets began to take on the look and power of later classes of 2-8-8-2s. As built, the tenders carried only 16 tons of coal and 12,000 gallons of water. But following a number of trips through the backshops, the Y-3s were outfitted with tenders that rode on six-wheel trucks and that were topped off with 30 tons of coal and 22,000 gallons of water. Total engine weight, compared to the Y-2a's, increased only from 526,000 to 539,000 pounds. With tractive effort at the rated 270 psi, boiler pressure was actually less—114,154 pounds compound versus 116,212 pounds compound for the Y-2s and Y-2a's. And finally the motive power department found a place under the running boards on the engineer's side for all those air pumps.

Most significant from a train-watcher's viewpoint was the addition of crossed handrails on the pilot deck, an enhancement that all future Y's would have. They were the brainchild of mechanical engineer Pilcher, who believed they would contribute to safety and also be decorative. They distinguished N&W 2-8-8-2s from everybody else's articulateds thereafter.

Right from the time they were delivered, the locomotives were given a whole new set of numbers whose first digit would be the same for all future Y's: namely "2." Forty-five of the Y-3s, numbered 2000-2044, were built by ALCO's Schenectady plant; the remaining five, 2045-2049, were Baldwin products. Pleased with the performance of the Y-3s, the N&W ordered 30 almost identical Mallets, except for larger tenders, from ALCO's Richmond Works. They were numbered 2050-2079, classified Y-3a, and built in 1923.

With freight traffic steadily increasing during the "Roaring Twenties," the N&W received an additional ten 2-8-8-2s numbered 2080-2089 from ALCO's

William E. Warden Coll.

More powerful than a Y? Well, yes, in some respects Z-1b class 2-6-6-2 No. 1442 could outperform the first Y's. But they were no match for the tractive effort of the subsequent Y's. Still, N&W purchased 190 of the 2-6-6-2s from ALCO and Baldwin between 1912 and 1916.

Richmond plant in 1927. Originally designed Y-3b, they were later reclassified Y-4. They boasted a total engine weight of 567,000 pounds, of which 508,500 pounds rested on the 58-inch drivers. Boiler pressure was 270 psi. The Y-4s were distinctive in several ways: They were the first compound locomotives with superheaters that N&W had purchased from commercial builders; they were the first N&W Mallets to have forward-slanting ("sports model") cabs, and five (or all, depending on which "authoritative source" is consulted) were equipped in 1948 with former Atlantic Coast Line tenders having eight-wheel trucks plus coal and water capacities of 27 tons and 24,000 gallons, respectively. Finally, they were the last new steam locomotives obtained by the N&W from anywhere but its own Roanoke Shops.

Following completion of the last Y-4, N&W saw the first few rays of the dawn of the day of steam "Superpower." All future N&W 2-8-8-2s were built with the same boiler pressure, weight on drivers, driver diameter, and tractive effort, but added features that would constantly improve the speed, efficiency, and serviceability of the Mallet locomotive. Considerable irony is involved here for these feeble rays of a new dawn were cast in the United States' darkest economic period. The year was 1930 and the country was sinking into the depth of the Great Depression.

Why did the N&W have the temerity—or foolishness—to build more Mallets, stopping not just with 10 in 1930 but adding nine in 1931 and one in 1932—this last in a year when no new locomotive orders were received by Baldwin, Lima, or ALCO. Part of the reason, historians will point out, is that stockbrokers may have been jumping out of windows in October 1929, but the nation's economy did not strike bottom until 1932; then too, the 10 steamers built in 1930 were planned and ordered in the boom year of 1929. Another part of the reason was that N&W, unlike most railroads in the Depression, continued to earn money. It never once skipped a dividend on its common stock. But even the N&W, cash rich because of a continuing need for coal plus stringent cost reductions in the 1920s, could hardly justify new locomotive construction in 1931 and 1932 solely on economic grounds.

So what was the rest of the reason? This subject was covered in detail in the author's book *Norfolk and Western A and J Class Locomotives* (Andover Junction Publications, 1987). A brief summary here will suffice. N&W had a team of skilled designers and workers who, experience had shown, could develop and build locomotives superior to anything that could come out of Schenctady, Lima, or Eddystone. Keeping this team on the payroll was less costly than trying to reassemble it when the economy picked up; hence the company would be ready to build new locomotives as soon as the need arose. In the meantime it used the accumulated knowledge and experience of this team to develop new locomotive designs that continued to make N&W among the most profitable railroads.

Thus, N&W President W. J. Jenks commenting in his 1939 Christmas message to employees on that autumn's traffic buildup could say, "So far as the future is concerned, I think we can look forward to the New Year with some degree of confidence. The Norfolk & Western has ample reserve capacity in modern equipment...to handle any further increase in business."

So it was that N&W's Y-5 class Mallets were built. Originally numbered 2090-2109, all but one acquired new numbers after undergoing modernization. This loner, No. 2092, had the misfortune of being destroyed in a boiler explosion at Maybeury, West

Virginia, in 1937.

The Y-5s' boilers generated steam at the then unheard-of 300 psi. Excluding a few experimental models, no contemporary American steam locomotive's boiler pressure reached this figure. No production locomotive carried a higher pressure until 1937 when Lima and Baldwin delivered 2-10-4s with 310 psi to Kansas City Southern and Santa Fe, respectively.

Combined with the high boiler pressure was an engine weight of 582,900 pounds, of which 522,850 was on the sixteen 58-inch drivers. Grate area, 96 or 97 square feet on previous Y's, was increased to 106 square feet. Cylinders remained 39" bore x 32" stroke forward and 25"x32" rear. The result was a phenomenal tractive effort of 152,206 pounds simple and 126,838 pounds compound, figures rivaled among contemporaries only by the Great Northern Railway's R-2 class simple 2-8-8-2s at 146,000 pounds, and Northern Pacific's Z-5 class simple 2-8-8-4's 153,440 pounds with boosters working (just 1,200 pounds more than the Y-5s). Only retention of inboard journal bearings permitted lineside observers to distinguish Y-5s from subsequent 2-8-8-2s.

Best of all, the Y-5 design finally licked the low-pressure cylinder back pressure problem. This feat was accomplished by employing 18-inch low-pressure exhaust valves, and by using a "bridge pipe" or "wishbone" as it was sometimes called. The latter device resembled a large inverted "Y." Its arms angled up from the low-pressure cylinder's exhausts, coming together to form the leg. The leg in turn was connected to the exhaust system. Medication that allows asthmatics to exhale more easily by expanding their bronchial passages works on a principle similar to that of the enlarged exhaust valves and bridge pipe. All subsequent Y's were built with this feature. Ultimately the Y-4s, and some Y-3s, were equipped with bridge pipes.

Then in 1936 the age of steam Superpower truly dawned brilliantly. On May 8 of that year, Roanoke Shops completed the first of its famed 2-6-6-4s, whose 70-inch drive wheels allowed them to power 14,000-ton manifests or protect passenger schedules with equal aplomb. Then on September 24, the first Y6 rolled off the Roanoke erecting floor. Management's thinking in the dark days of 1930 had finally paid off.

The Y-6 story is told beginning on page 25 and encompasses the balance of this book.

John Krause Coll.

Y-1 No. 1719 is creating vast amounts of smoke at some undisclosed location. The chronicles don't record the photographer's name or date, but it is surely in the mid-1920s.

No. 996 still in service in March 1924 at Roanoke, but time has run out—it was scrapped later that year. Note the obvious difference in size between the rear high-pressure cylinder and the forward low-pressure one. The dry-pipe supplying high-pressure steam to the rear engine is plainly visible leading down from the steam dome just forward of the bell.

H. K. Vollrath Coll.

2-8-8-2 (Y-Class) Locomotives of the Norfolk & Western Railway

Class	Number	Cylinders	Drivers Diam.	Boiler Press.	Wt. on Drivers/ Total Weight	Trac. Effort	Built	Builder	Tender Gal./Tons (Note 6)
Y-1	995-999	24-1/2x30(H) 39x30(L)	56	200psi	370,000/400,000	66,892(C) 83,615(S)	1910	Baldwin	9,000/14
Y-2	1700,1701	24-1/2x32(H) 39x32(L)	56	230psi	472,000/526,000	104,300(C) 123,960(S)	1918	Roanoke	12,000/20
	1702						1919	Roanoke	
	1703,1704						1921	Roanoke	
	1711-1730						1919	Baldwin	
Y-2a	1705-1710	25x32(H) 39x32(L)	57	270psi	472,000/526,000	116,212(C) 139,450(S)	1924	Roanoke	12,000/20
Y-3	2000-2044	25x32(H) 39x32(L)	57	270psi	485,000/539,000	114,154(C) 136,985(S)	1919	ALCO-Schenectady	12,000/16
	2045-2049						1919	Baldwin	
Y-3a	2050-2079 (Note 1)	25x32(H) 39x32(L)	57	270psi	485,000/539,000	114,154(C) 136,985(S)	1923	ALCO-Richmond	15,000/17
Y-4	2080-2089 (Note 2)	25x32(H) 39x32(L)	58	270psi	508,500/567,000	114,154(C) 136,985(S)	1927	ALCO-Richmond	16,000/23
Y-5	2090-2099	25x32(H) 39x32(L)	58	300psi	522,850/582,900	126,838(C) 152,206(S)	1930	Roanoke	22,000/26
	2100-2108						1931	Roanoke	
	2109 (Note3)						1932	Roanoke	
Y-6	2120-2124	25x32(H) 39x32(L)	58 (Note 4)	300psi	522,850/582,900	126,838(C) 152,206(S)	1936	Roanoke	22,000/26 (Note 5)
	2125,2126						1937	Roanoke	
	2127-2134						1938	Roanoke	
	2135-2143						1939	Roanoke	
	2144-2154						1940	Roanoke	
Y-6a	2155-2170	25x32(H) 39x32(L)	58	300psi	522,850/582,900	126,838C) 152,206(S)	1942	Roanoke	22,000/30
Y-6b	2171-2180	25x32(H) 39x32(L)	58	300psi	522,850/582,900 (Note 7)	126,838(C) 152,206(S)	1948	Roanoke	22,000/30
	2181-2187						1949	Roanoke	
	2188-2193						1950	Roanoke	
	2194-2196						1951	Roanoke	
	2197-2200						1952	Roanoke	

Notes:

Note 1 - The following Y-3a's were ultimately equipped with tenders taken from scrapped Bessemer & Lake Erie 2-10-4s: 2055, 2056, 2058, 2061, 2071, 2079.

Note 2 - All Y-4s were initially classified Y-3b, but classification was changed shortly after delivery. In 1948 Y-4s were equipped with ex-Atlantic Coast Line eight-axle tenders with capacity of 27,000 gallons/27 tons.

(Continued on next page)

Legend
H= High-pressure Cylinders
L= Low-pressure cylinders
C= Working compound
S= Working simple

Note 3 - Some Y-5s rebuilt in 1941 with cast frames, roller bearings, and 300psi boiler pressure, and renumbered. Old and new numbers as follows:

Old	New
2094	2110
2090	2111
2098	2112
2096	2113
2095	2114
2100	2115
2091	2116
2097	2117
2099	2118
2093	2119

All rebuilt Y-5s kept inboard bearings on the pilot and trailing trucks.

Note 4 - Y-5s as originally built had 57-inch drivers.

Note 5 - Y-6 tender size *as built*. Tender capacity later increased to 22,000 gallons/30 tons.

Note 6 - Engine data taken from N&W Motive Power Department specifications; tender data taken from LaMassena, Robert A., *Articulated Steam Locomotives of North America* (Sundance Books 1979), and represents the capacities of original tenders. Capacities of tenders assigned to locomotives in the late 1940s and 1950s are as follows:

Class	Gallons water	Tons coal
Y-2	18,000	26
Y-2a	18,000	26
Y-3	22,000	30
Y-3a	22,000	30
Y-4	22,000	30 (see Note 2)
Y-5	22,000	30
Y-6	22,000	30
Y-6a	22,000	30
Y-6b	22,000	30

Note 7 - When the additional ballast was added to the Y-6b (see page 25) the weights changed to 548,500 on drivers and 611,520 total.

N&W photo, W. E. Warden Coll.

A Y-class boiler under construction at Roanoke Shops, probably in the late 1930s. Some idea of the enormity of the firebox can be had by comparing it to the size of the men standing around and in it.

N&W photo, W. E. Warden Coll.

N&W RY.
PRECISION
TRANSPORTATION

Engineer W. J. Fielding adjusts the sander of a 2-8-8-2 on the Radford Division back in 1938.

William E. Warden

In this archetypical steam-age scene, the engineer of Y-4 No. 2083 oils a rear side rod bearing at Waynesboro, Virginia, in April 1957, while waiting for a green board to proceed with his local freight. This 1927 Richmond Locomotive Works product was one of the first Y's to receive the slanted front "sports model" cab. The pipes attached to the firebox are condensing coils for removing moisture from the air brake line.

N&W's Wandering Y's

Most Class I railroads' "workhorses" eventually were sold, usually to some cash-strapped short line, while there was still some useful life left in them. Thus Baltimore & Ohio might sell obsolete 2-8-0s to the Buffalo Creek & Gauley or Southern Railway dispose of elderly 2-8-2s to Tennesee Central. N&W treated its workhorses in a similar manner, except for one difference. But then, as we have already seen, N&W was different from other railroads. That difference even applied to disposing of surplus 2-8-8-2s. Thus, many were sold to such giants as the Santa Fe, Union Pacific, and Pennsylvania.

Most, if not all, were used during World War II to relieve motive power shortages on other rail lines that, unlike N&W, had not built and stockpiled locomotives during the lean years of the 1930s. This stockpiling had made most of the Y-2s and many of the Y-3s obsolete—by contemporary N&W standards, that is—and it was these older Mallets that became the N&W's wandering 2-8-8-2s. Herewith then, some notes on these Y's that left N&W rails during the 1940s to fight World War II on another front.

Bingham & Garfield Railway

If the name Bingham & Garfield sounds foreign to you, how about Kennecott Copper Corporation? For indeed the copper mining giant operated the B&G, with just 16 miles of main line, as its own. These 16 miles connected a copper mine in Bingham Canyon, Utah, some 20 miles from Salt Lake City, with a smelter at Garfield.

Copper was a high-priority item during World War II. To help move the vastly increased production of copper ore being mined in Bingham Canyon, the B&G in June 1943 purchased N&W Y-2s Nos. 1721 and 1723 and renumbered them respectvely 109 and 110 (later renumbered again to 400 and 401). Once in Utah, the former Y-2s joined eight ALCO-built 0-8-8-0 Mallets in hustling ore trains from the mine to the Garfield smelter. Both 0-8-8-0s and the 2-8-8-2s were scrapped around 1948 when the B&G's main line was electrified.

Atchison, Topeka & Santa Fe

Paupa, Rabaul, Guadalcanal. These flyspecks of islands that most people never heard of were suddenly on everyone's mind in early 1943, as the war in the Pacific heated up and both the Japanese and the Allies threw tens of thousands of men and huge amounts of materiel into the fight for control of these strategic outposts. Suddenly the Santa Fe, as well as other western railroads, found themselves hauling unexpectedly large quantities of troops and munitions to San Diego, San Francisco, and other Pacific Coast ports for shipment to battlefields half a world away.

Although the Santa Fe's experience with articulateds generally had been less than encouraging up to that point (it rebuilt its last Mallets into 2-10-2s during the First World War, mostly because of poor designs), the railroad's expanded wartime traffic, coupled with heavy grades and availability of surplus N&W Y-3s, left it with few alternatives. Between July and October 1943, the Santa Fe received eight of the Mallets.

Removing the brakeman's shanty (commonly called the "doghouse") from the tender tops, Santa Fe put these boomer 2-8-8-2s to work on one of the road's worst grades: Raton Pass. The Y-3s dug in and did a commendable job pushing freight—after all, that was their specialty—up Raton's 3-percent grade. They even doubleheaded with the Santa Fe's 2900-series 4-8-4s on the head of such name trains as *The Chief* when the swollen consists proved too much for the 4-8-4s' 80-inch drivers.

Despite this good record, the Santa Fe was less than satisfied with the Mallets. They were too slow going downgrade and getting out of the way of the next train. That had never been a problem on Blue Ridge grade either before, during, or after the war; high-speed traffic density was just that much heavier on Santa Fe than on the N&W. No matter; the Santa Fe bought no more N&W locomotives, and in 1947 sold the surviving 2-8-8-2s back east to the Virginian Railway.

Denver & Rio Grande Western

Perhaps because of its experience with its own 4-6-6-4s on Tennessee Pass and other daunting grades, the Rio Grande bore no prejudice against articulateds. But whatever the reason, the D&RGW grabbed up four surplus N&W Y-2s in April 1943, making it the first road to purchase the 2-8-8-2s. It bought two more in June of that year and another two in August. Then, with the war in Europe winding down and most military attention being turned to the Pacific theatre, the Rio Grande purchased a final seven Y-2s and Y-2a's in May 1945.

Just why the Rio Grande stuck with the Y-2/Y-2a's instead of buying some of the newer Y-3s in 1945, is a matter of conjecture. Most likely that, from a spare parts viewpoint, the mountain road considered it wiser to have 13 nearly identical 2-8-8-2s rather than seven of one class and six of another. Then too, the Y-2s were quite similar in design to the Rio Grande's own USRA 2-8-8-2s. The road did, however, also purchase four of the N&W's poorly-designed K-3 class 4-8-2s so there may have been other considerations involved. Whatever the reason, some imported Mallets were still on the premises as late as 1950.

Information on where the Y-2s were employed

is somewhat sketchy. Tennessee Pass, where 4-6-6-4s were regularly used as helpers, and Moffat Tunnel were two of their early assignments. The imposing Rocky Mountain landscape may have been startlingly different from Blue Ridge, but the grades and the job to be done were not.

C. W. Burns, W. E. Warden Coll.

The distinctive crossed handrails on the pilot deck of Union Pacific No. 3673 are a dead giveaway to its origin as N&W Y-3 No. 2041. Shown here at Cheyenne, Woming, in 1946, a long way from its familiar haunts on the Blue Ridge of Virginia.

Pennsylvania Railroad

Whether the Pennsylvania purchased surplus Y's from the N&W or simply asked for them to be delivered is a fair subject for speculation. After all, the PRR owned more than a third of the N&W's common stock at the time and could pretty much have its own way with the smaller road. Regardless of the reason, the PRR came into possession of six surplus Y-3s in May 1943. Despite having tried out one of the N&W's 2-6-6-4s and possessing formidable grades of its own, the Pennsylvania never did like articulateds. It preferred to entrust its heavy wartime traffic to Altoona-built J-1 class 2-10-4s, plus purely drag-freight I-1s-class Santa Fe type 2-10-0s dating back to 1916, and M-1 class 4-8-2s introduced in 1923.

But Altoona could not keep pace with the burgeoning traffic. The first 2-10-4 wasn't completed until 1942, and there were places that the 2-10-0s needed help. Given these circumstances, PRR management could be open-minded about allowing second-hand articulateds on the property. Thus it was that N&W Mallets could be found at such as Enola and on the Harrisburg-Hagerstown branch. The southern end of this branch butted up against the beginning of the N&W's Shenandoah Division. Hence it is possible that these locomotives were sometimes on track adjacent to the same engines with which they had once shared the roundhouse at Shenandoah or Roanoke.

One interesting sidelight: The Y-3s were equipped with PRR's distinctive keystone number plates on their smokebox doors. The keystones were normally reserved for passenger engines and PRR's only other purely freight engines to wear them were the J-1-class 2-10-4s. Quite an honor for 24-year-old second-hand locomotives.

Union Pacific

Union Pacific also had no biases against articulateds; its Challengers and Big Boys were probably as well known to train watchers as were N&W's Y's and A's. So when wartime traffic destined for West Coast ports strained the resources of UP's motive power department, what was more natural than to turn to N&W for help?

UP was not easily strained as it stabled some of the most modern motive power in the United States. Hence, it was not until June 1945 that the road took delivery of just five Y-3s. Given typical Union Pacific train indicator boards, the Y-3s (if you ignored the spoked pilot and trailing-truck wheels) looked a bit like scaled-down versions of the Big Boys. Most of the Y-3s' service on the UP was spent working around Green River and Rock Springs, Wyoming, places far removed both by distance and topography from the lush green hills of Virginia, but still ideally suited for the 2-8-8-2s' talents.

Athough the Y-3s were great for helping out in a pinch, they were no match for the high-stepping Challengers and Big Boys with fast freights. All former N&W Mallets were scrapped in 1948. They did, however, outlast the speedier Chesapeake & Ohio single-expansion 2-8-8-2s that UP also had purchased in 1945.

Virginian Railway

The Virginian's seven Y's didn't quite fit the mold of the other wandering Y's; they weren't bought second-hand but rather third-hand from Santa Fe. Neither were they acquired during World War II, but rather in December 1947, when the nation was in the midst of its first postwar economic boom and the Virginian wanted to retire some of its aging (1918) 2-10-10-2s. The boomer Y-3s weren't placed into service until mid-1948, following overhauls at Virginian's Princeton, West Virginia, shops. But it was the first time VGN ever bought used steam locomotives and the company wanted to be sure its investment in the seven locomotives was served.

Hauling mine-run tonnage was the Y-3s' principal occupation on the Virginian, an occupation with which the 2-8-8-2s had considerable experience. They supplemented the road's own West End (that is, west of Roanoke) power until the Virginian received its first Fairbanks-Morse Trainmaster diesels in early 1954.

Summary Roster of The Wandering Y's

Railroad	Road No.	Date Acquired	N&W Class/No.	Railroad	Road No.	Date Acquired	N&W Class/No.
Bingham & Garfield	109(400)	June 1943	Y-2/1721	Pennsylvania	373	May 1943	Y-3/2000
	110(401)	June 1943	Y-2/1723		374	May 1943	Y-3/2008
					375	May 1943	Y-3/2027
					376	May 1943	Y-3/2034
AT&SF	1790	Oct. 1943	Y-3/2021		377	May 1943	Y-3/2036
	1791	Oct. 1943	Y-3/2022		378	May 1943	Y-3/2046
	1792	Oct. 1943	Y-3/2015				
	1793	Oct. 1943	Y-3/2026	Union Pacific	3670	June 1945	Y-3/2030
	1794	Oct. 1943	Y-3/2014		3671	June 1945	Y-3/2020
	1795	Oct. 1943	Y-3/2029		3672	June 1945	Y-3/2025
	1796	July 1943	Y-3/2035		3673	June 1945	Y-3/2041
	1797	? 1943	Y-3/2042		3674	June 1945	Y-3/2013
D&RGW	3550	April 1943	Y-2/1701	Virginian	736	Dec. 1947	Y-3/2014
	3551	April 1943	Y-2/1722		737	Dec. 1947	Y-3/2015
	3552	April 1943	Y-2/1724		738	Dec. 1947	Y-3/2021
	3553	April 1943	Y-2/1728		739	Dec. 1947	Y-3/2022
	3554	June 1943	Y-2/1729		740	Dec. 1947	Y-3/2026
	3555	June 1943	Y-2/1730		741	Dec. 1947	Y-3/2029
	3556	Aug. 1943	Y-2a/1710		742	Dec. 1947	Y-3/2035
	3557	Aug. 1943	Y-2/1727				
	3558	May 1945	Y-2a/1706				
	3559	May 1945	Y-2a/1709				
	3560	May 1945	Y-2/1713				
	3561	May 1945	Y-2/1714				
	3562	May 1945	Y-2/1719				
	3563	May 1945	Y-2/1725				
	3564	May 1945	Y-2/1726				

Note: Virginian locomotives were third-hand via AT&SF.

Former N&W Y-2 No. 1724 is seen here as D&RGW No. 3552 shoving a string of ore hoppers upgrade near Mitchell, Colorado, on September 3, 1949. The built-up coal bunker and "flying logo" of the Rio Grade are among the few changes evident.

(both) Ross Grenard

D&RGW No. 3552 is again seen, in company with one of the road's own simple articulateds, switching at Tenessee Pass, Colorado. The photographer states that this is probably "as high an elevation as was ever attained by an N&W engine." — No argument here.

Otto Perry photo, Ed Crist Coll.

A triple-header, rare on any railroad, was far from common on the Santa Fe. What makes this photo even more unusual is that the locomotive in the lead is AT&SF No. 1797, formerly N&W No. 2042. The train is *The Caifornia Limited*, taken in January 16, 1944, near Lynn, New Mexico.

(Right) ex-N&W No. 2021, lettered Santa Fe No. 1790, is shown at Elkhart, Indiana, a site far removed from either railroad, as it is shipped back to the hills and hollows of West Virginia and Virginia; only this time it'll be on the Virginian Railway's roster. **(Below)** Virginian No. 740, formerly N&W Y-3 No. 2026 (and AT&SF No. 1793) rests at the Elmore, West Virginia engine house in August 1949.

C. W. Jernstrom, W. E. Warden Coll.

H. Reid

Y-2 Photos

(Above) This 24-year-old Y-2, No. 1705, had its coal bunker topped off for business in Roanoke yard in August 1948. ***(Center)*** N&W Motive Power Department diagram for the Y-2 shows it to be 110 feet long over the coupler pulling faces, with a wheelbase of 57 feet, 4 inches and rigid wheelbase of each engine 15 feet, 6 inches. ***(Bottom)*** This right side view of Y-2 No. 1700 shows the first of the class waiting on Roanoke yard to begin the day's shifting activity. Not many railroads had switchers with this much muscle!

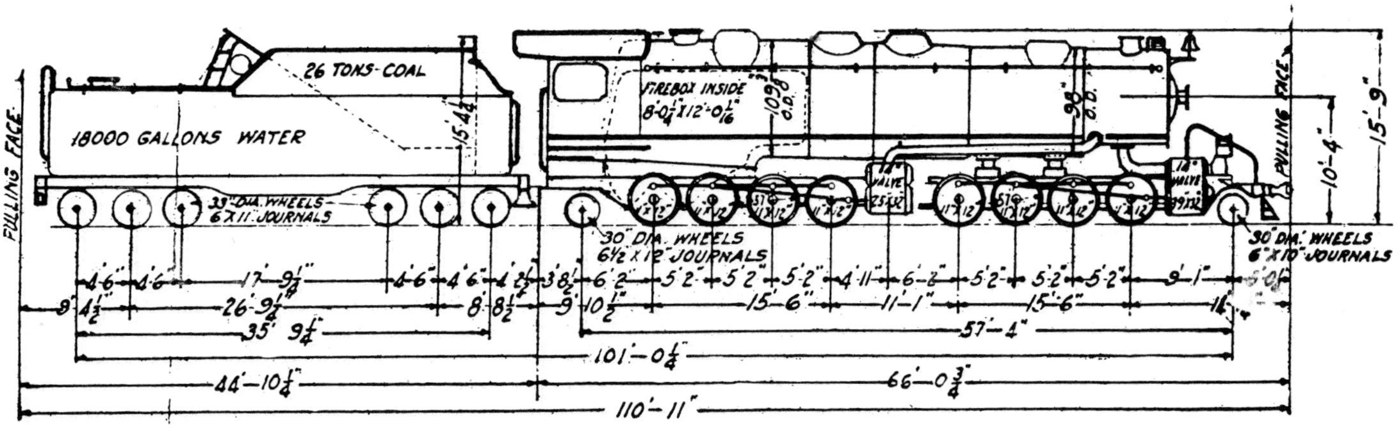

(both photos) J. R. Quinn Coll.

Y-3 Photos

W. R. Baumgardner, Jr. Coll.

New at ALCO's Schenectady works in 1919, N&W Y-3 No. 2009 poses with a faceful of air pumps. A later modification tucked the pumps under the running board, but bells remained atop the smokebox; later classes of Y's had the bell to the rear, near the cab.

Joe Schmitz

(Above) Y-3 No. 2009 still turning an honest dollar for the N&W as a switcher at Portsmouth, Ohio's huge yard in July 1957. ***(Below)*** Mechanical diagram of Y-3 with 30-ton/22,000-gallon tender, and measuring almost 15 feet, 9 inches from top of rail to top of stack.

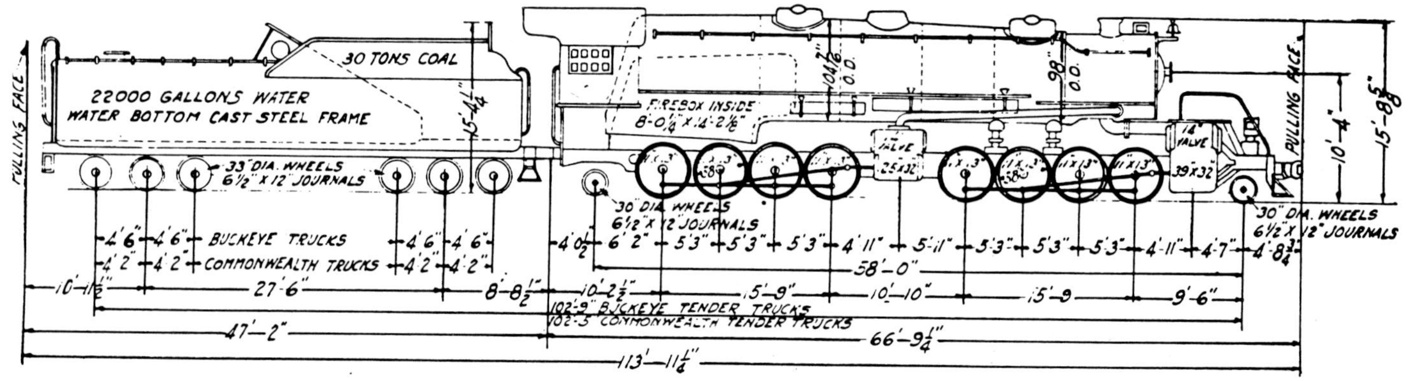

An eastbound coal drag behind Y-3a No. 2064 passes a westbound merchandise freight near Elliston, Virginia, about 1940 in a superb company photograph. This is likely a posed photo, with a squirrel-tail wisp of steam exhausting from each locomotive airbrushed in to give the impression of speed. But nonetheless a great photo in a beautiful sweeping vista of the Roanoke Valley.

N&W photo, W. E. Warden Coll.

Second trick (shift) crews in a lamentably unidentified yard line up in front of their engines in the winter of 1956-57. At left is S-1 class 0-8-0 No. 222, and at right Y-3 No. 2042. Despite the disparity in size between the two locomotives, they will perform similar duties this day.

N&W Photo, Robert D. Simpson Coll.

Y-3a No.2069 crosses a trestle over the Clinch River on the coal-rich Bluefield-Norton line in southwest Virginia, with a string of empty hoppers in the summer of 1954. Not much water under the trestle, indicating a dry summer.

John Krause, T. W. Dixon Coll.

Railroad Avenue Enterprises Coll.

Y-3 No. 2040 shoves hard on a cut of loaded hopper cars in Bluefield in the early-mid-1950s.

Jim Shaw

Occasionally the Y's shared the glory with A-class 2-6-6-4s out on the Scioto Division. But Y-3 No. 2037, easing a cut of empty hoppers around a curve in Portsmouth, Ohio, is definitely playing a supporting role, although certainly an essential one, in April 1956.

Y-4 Photos

H. Reid

Back in 1947, 30-year-old Y-4 No. 2082 will be ready to haul an extra out of Roanoke yard as soon as the engineer completes his oiling and inspection chores.

Having finished with the side rod, Y-4 No. 2083's engineer is now applying oil to the left rear valve gear. In another ten minutes a northbound manifest freight out on the main line will pass 2083, the engineer will then stow his oil can and get back to the business of jockeying power reverse, throttle, and sander. Photographed in April 1956 at Waynesboro, Virginia.

William E. Warden

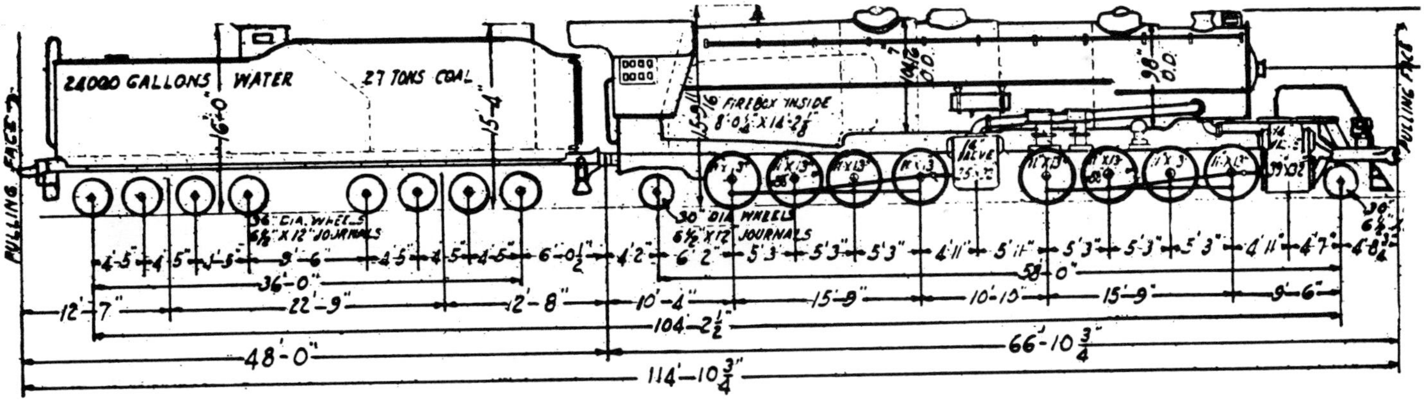

N&W Motive Power Department diagram of the Y-4 class, with a 27-ton/24,000-gallon tender.

N&W photo, Robert D. Simpson Coll.

(Above) Basset Furniture Company of Basset, Virginia, on N&W's Winston-Salem line is one of the railroad's long-time customers. In October 1939, Y-4 No. 2098 with a southbound merchandise freight train pauses in front of the furniture plant's loading dock to pick up loaded cars. Much of the furniture is constructed from locally-cut walnut, oak, and poplar.

(Right) A southbound local freight behind Y-4 No. 2083 whips around a curve at Crimora, Virginia, in June 1956. The 2083, a 1927 product of ALCO's Richmond Locomotive Works, spent most of the mid-1950s working on the Shenandoah Division, but when that line was dieselized, was promoted to working locals between Roanoke and Lynchburg.

William E. Warden

Y-5 Photos

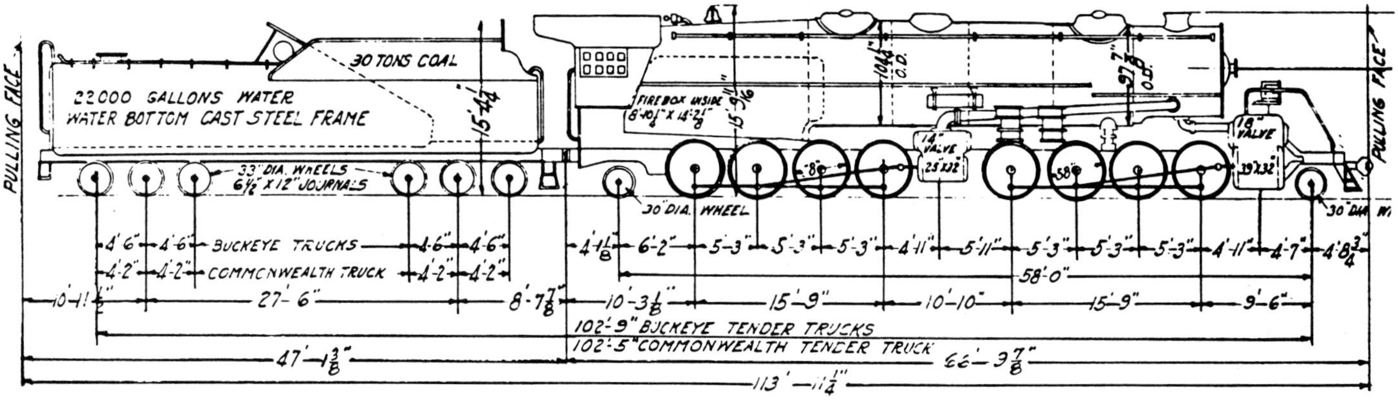

(Above) Official N&W diagram shows Y-5 class, its plump boiler measuring 104-1/4 inches at the second course and almost 98 at the last, just behind the smokebox.

Bruce D. Fales, T. W. Dixon Coll.

(Left) Y-5 No. 2100 moves forward at the N&W's Hagerstown yard in 1935. N&W's Shenandoah Division ran from Roanoke northeast to Hagerstown where connections were made with the Western Maryland and Pennsylvania railroads.

J. R. Quinn

Y-5 No. 2116 (No. 2091 before being rebuilt with cast steel frame and roller bearings) waits in Cincinnati's Clare Yard to power an eastbound extra in August 1948.

(Left) Y-5 No. 2120 thunders through Pamplin, Virginia, with an extra move in this July 1948 scene. Although in later days the area around Pamplin would be considered almost the exclusive province of 2-6-6-4 A-Class, ten of the A's still remain to be built at this date, and besides, a road foreman of engines tied whatever was handy on the front of an extra.

(Below) Y-5 No. 2115 wheels an extra around a curve near Waverly, Virginia, in July 1948. Waverly, it is said, was named by Otelia, wife of General Billy Mahone, builder of N&W's predecessor Atlantic, Mississippi & Ohio. The lady was a great fan of novelist Sir Walter Scott and in his honor we got Waverly, Wakefield, Ivor, and Zuni.

(both) J. R. Quinn

Zenith of the 2-8-8-2 - The Y-6

The Y-6s were Y-5s with a difference. No attempt was made to build a more powerful 2-8-8-2; the Y-5s were judged to have as much strength as a 2-8-8-2 would ever need. Rather, emphasis was placed on ease and economy of fabrication, decreasing downtime needed for servicing and increasing fuel economy to the practical limit for reciprocating steam locomotives.

In common with the A-class 2-6-6-4 simple articulateds, Y-6s were built with cast steel beds (actually separate castings for front and rear drivers connected by means of a pin hinge and with a combined weight of 106,500 pounds) and outside frame bearings on lead and trailing trucks (which certainly improved the latter's appearance). The cast steel beds were only added to the design after they proved so successful on the A's.

All journals were equipped with roller bearings. Drive wheels were 57 inches in diameter (later increased to 58). Automatic lubrication for cylinders, steam chests, guides, and a total of 213 moving parts, was supplied by lubricators actuated by the valve gear. This and roller bearings cut maintenance time and expense, thereby minimizing downtime to the point where the Y-6 was competitive with the best diesels of the era. Maximum horsepower was ultimately an astounding 5,500, reached at 25 mph. And although the Y-6s and subsequent subclasses were hampered by a top speed of around 50 mph, they could roll up an average of 6,000 miles of revenue service per month. So successful was the Y-6 design that eventually the Y-5s also were given roller bearings and automatic lubrication, although for reasons obscure, pilot and trailing trucks were left with inside bearings.

Before the end of steam, two subclasses of the Y-6 were built, both virtually identical on the outside to the original Y-6s. Replacing the Worthington BL-model pump on the left side, a recessed Worthington type SA feedwater heater in the Y-6b's smokebox was its distinguishing feature. The recessed heater plus a hot water pump under the smokebox caused the earlier Y-6b's to be built with oval smokebox doors, thereby limiting access to the inside. Eventually design modifications were made to these Y-6b's to retrofit them with conventional round doors. The Y-6s and Y-6a's were best distinguished by their engine numbers.

But on the inside, the Y-6b's were considerably modified. The combustion chamber just forward of the firebox was increased from 42 to 84 inches. Additionally, as we mentioned earlier, the semi-automatic reducing valve, which allowed high-pressure steam into the low-pressure cylinders on starting was replaced with one controlled by the engineer. This last change allowed the engineer to accelerate to any desired speed before switching to compound operation. Other modifications included firebox circulator tubes and insulated smokeboxes.

Then late in the Y-6b's production cycle, that booster valve spoken of earlier was added to permit a shot of high-pressure superheated steam to flow through the pipe connecting the high- and low-pressure cylinders. It is said that the first Y-6b to receive the booster valve was No. 2197, outshopped just before the 1952 diesel-verses-steam tests (see page 33). This "supercharging" so increased tractive effort that it was necessary to add 13 tons of lead to the engine frame to prevent the drivers from slipping. It is said also that No. 2197's boiler pressure was also increased from 300 to 315 psi for the tests, but N&W management never acknowledged this.

Roanoke finally outshopped the N&W's last articulated steam locomotive, Y-6b 2200, in 1952, three years after the last commercial locomotive builder in the United States exited the business.

Jenks' 1939 Christmas remarks about the road's reserve capacity for "further increase in business" may have been an understatement, or he simply may have recognized what inevitably lay ahead. Two years later, with the United States involved in World War II, N&W traffic soared, and by 1943 N&W had the heaviest traffic density of any American railroad (measured by ton-mile per mile of railroad).

Blame Hitler's U-boats lurking off the Atlantic coast for much of this increase. Freight that previously went to New York, Baltimore, and other ports by water now had to travel inland as far north as possible, and N&W's Shenandoah Division was the only north-south route east of the Alleghanies that didn't go through Richmond, Fredricksburg & Potomac's traffic-clogged Potomac Yard. Four through freights in each direction were scheduled between Roanoke and Hagerstown. But suddenly harried dispatchers were clearing as many as 10 sections of each train out of Roanoke. Almost all this new freight was moving behind 2-8-8-2s. Straining gritty Ys in front and behind moved solid coal trains averaging 6,000 tons over the division's saw-tooth profile during the war years. And all this had to be sandwiched in between the division's four daily passenger trains and as many as 16 troop extras every 24 hours.

President Jenks, incidentally, suddenly found himself a full colonel in the U. S. Army at age 73. To prevent a threatened railroad strike by several operating unions over wages, the Federal Government seized the railroads on December 27, 1943, but settlement of disputes allowed them to be returned to civilian control on January 18, 1944, after only three weeks under army administration. The N&W's president was inducted into the Army and appointed director of the Pocahontas Region, returning to civilian status at the conclusion of the seizure. The N&W didn't win World War II single-handedly, of course, but Jenks' foresight in building and rebuilding locomotives for which there was no immediate need during the Depression years arguably shortened the conflict.

In the early 1950s with the world (discounting Korea) more or less at peace, performance of the Y's, as well as the A's, was improved even further. Downtime for servicing could be reduced and gross ton-miles-per-train-hour increased, if some of the steamers' frequent stops for water were eliminated, particularly if a water stop had to be made while a train was heading upgrade.

The improvement was simple. Auxiliary water tanks, familiarly known as "canteens," were tacked behind the regular tenders. Consisting of tenders saved from older Mallets and scrapped engines of other railroads, the canteens carried an additional 16,000 to 24,000 gallons of water, thereby eliminating the need for 17 water stops systemwide and extending appreciably the distance a train could travel before its locomotive needed to stop for a drink. The result was a 31-percent increase in gross ton-miles-per-train-hour, and the Y-5s and Y-6s had reached 89,152 gross ton-miles-per-train-hour in September 1956, much of it in drag service plus helper duties on Blue Ridge grade. (A helper leaving Boaz helper siding near Vinton, just east of Roanoke, journeying to Blue Ridge, then returning to Boaz, made a round trip of just 20 miles, but a helper might make this same round trip a dozen times in 24 hours.) N&W Mechanical Inspector W. O. Hunt, Jr., in an address to the Norton (Virginia) Better Service Club in November 1956 summed up this astounding performance succinctly: "The amount of work accomplished by these machines [Y's and A's] is hard to comprehend."

One more innovation to reduce downtime was added in 1955: new engine terminals at Bluefield, Williamson and seven other locations that permited complete servicing—cleaning fire, lubrication, watering, washing, coaling, sanding, inspection, and turning a Y-6 on a turntable—all in less than 90 minutes. The N&W had, in the words of one rail writer, "Dieselized without ever purchasing a diesel."

Another bit of fine tuning took place in the early 1950s but even the most observant train watcher would have been unaware of it. There had been problems with reducing valves sticking when the engineer furnished low-pressure cylinders with high-pressure boiler steam. The sticking was finally solved but the resulting changes caused the front engine to slip. To end this slipping some 25,600 pounds of lead were poured into hollow portions of the cast steel beds.

The Y-6s and their fat-boilered sisters could not halt dieselization forever, no more than could the A's and J's. Needed spare parts that Roanoke couldn't fabricate were becoming difficult to obtain by the mid-1950s; the price of coal was rising (they didn't get the stuff for free, even from on-line coal companies) relative to oil, many steamers were reaching the end of their useful lives, and those remaining were mostly too big and powerful to be used efficiently on lightly trafficked branch lines. (At least one rail author has theorized that the Pennsylvania Railroad, which then owned 33-percent of N&W's common stock, had a hand in its dieselization. While this may be true, there is no documentation to support the theory and this author is inclined to discount it.)

Diesels first invaded the Lynchburg-Durham line in 1955, displacing aging 2-6-6-2s, which N&W maintained it needed to carry increased traffic on the main line. In 1957 the Shenandoah Division, long a 2-8-8-2 stronghold, was dieselized. The motive power score in 1954 was 444 to zero in favor of steam; it was 346 to 170 as 1958 dawned. But where there were mountains to climb, the Ys remained in command. A trio of EMD GP9 diesels might sometimes take over helper duties on Blue Ridge grade, but in 1958 they were still the exception. Save for locals, Y's shoved on the rear of virtually every eastbound freight and shared head-end duties with the A's.

This Mallet, this anachronism of a steam locomotive, with its 300 pounds of superheated steam, roller bearings, automatic lubrication, and auxiliary water tank, was still holding at bay the best that Electro-Motive Division, ALCO, and Baldwin had to offer. The EMD GP9s and the ALCO RS-11s kept coming, however. And as they did, the compounds began retreating into the hills and hollows of Appalachian coal country where, like cornered animals, they made their last stand. Relatively new Y-6s lost their road pilots in favor of footboards for working mine runs to such places as War, Jenkinjones, and other colorfully-named West Virginia communities.

Finally, on May 6, 1960, the last N&W steam road locomotive in service, Y-6b No. 2190, dropped its fire for the final time. And on September 30, 1960, the N&W removed from the roster its remaining operable steam locomotives—S-1a-class 0-8-0s 206, 215, 217, 231, 234 and 235; Y-6s 2132, 2134, 2153, and 2154, and Y-6b 2188, all of which were then stationed at Williamson, West Virginia.

Today, only two of these splendid compound locomotives exist: Y-4 No. 2050 at the Illinois Railway Museum at Union, Illinois, and Y-6a No. 2156 at the National Museum of Transport in St. Louis. Once in a while, reports surface of a dilapidated 2-8-8-2 rusting on some remote rip track, a sort of flanged-wheeled Flying Dutchman. But at this writing [1993] it is many years since the last verified report of partially dismantled 2-8-8-2s was heard. These hapless engines, Nos. 2143 and 2174, were photographed at Roanoke's United Iron & Metal Company. When this company was sold to British interests in the mid-1970s the two engines were finally scrapped.

Will either of the museum Mallets ever steam again? Good question! Railfan groups have several times suggested putting No. 2156 back into operation for excursion trips but the Mallet has been parked in St. Louis since July 1959 and so far no one has come forth with the money for the necessary restoration. Were this author a betting man, he'd bet on the engines staying put.

But when old railroaders and train watchers talk of N&W's steam past, conversation inevitably gets around to the 2-8-8-2s. And many people knew, loved, and respected these monsters with their clanking rods, haunting whistles whose sound floated up from the Shenandoah and Roanoke valleys and echoed off the mountains, whose smoke plumes shot a hundred feet in the sky on Blue Ridge grade and sharp exhausts shouted defiance at the laws of gravity, as the ground shuddered underfoot, and the huge machines' headlights bored holes in midnight darkness. These men begin talking of their own recollections—perhaps hand-firing a Y-6 (a two-man job) when the automatic stoker failed. The Ys were a more personal thing than the A's and J's could ever be. The veterans will speak too, of the men who operated this powerful railway and its trains, yet still had time and uncommon courtesy to make a trackside visitor welcome. They will talk of such as Norfolk Division Assistant Trainmaster Walter Jackson, who could arrange with friendly engine crews to add a special fillip to their whistle blowing for the benefit of a young railfan intent on recording on tape the best of steam railroading.

If you were among those Heaven-blest who did know the Y's, may this book help you evoke your own recollections. And if you were not so blest, may this book help you understand why these Mallets were so special to the rest of us. Perhaps too, it will help you to understand why engineer Fred A. Whittaker, who signed on with the N&W as a fireman in the year of Pearl Harbor, could declare with conviction almost two decades later, "I had but a single wish [as a child] and that was to get on the railroad as a locomotive engineer." Or why engineer Alonza Carter, upon retiring in 1957 after 53 years with the N&W (did anyone ever work 53 years for General Electric or IBM in this century?) could say simply "I always wanted to run an engine."

Roanoke Against LaGrange - The 1952 Diesel vs. Steam Tests

That the immensely profitable N&W continued to ignore the diesel locomotive in the early 1950s must surely have distressed the corporate managers of General Motors' Electro-Motive Division, which had started as a diesel maker, and ALCO and Baldwin, both of which had switched from steam to diesels in the late 1940s. After all, most every other Class I railroad had embraced the diesel by that time as a drowning man most surely embraced a life preserver; yet most provided stockholders with nowhere near the return on investment the N&W did. Hence there must have been considerable crowing in GM's board room when, in 1952, the N&W allowed EMD to test its newest against the best and brightest of Roanoke Shops.

These tests have been discussed previously in other books, notably Ed King's *The A-Norfolk & Western's Mercedes of Steam* (Trans Anglo Books 1991), and this author's *Norfolk & Western: Diesel's Last Conquest* (TLC Publishing, 1991). Because of that, plus the fact that the outcome of the tests had negligible impact on the Y's future, readers are presented with only a brief review of the tests. Contestants in this battle of internal combustion against superheated steam were as follows: For Electro-Motive Division: F7 model four-unit diesel No. 459, rated at 6,000 crankshaft horsepower––and for N&W: A-class 2-6-6-4 No. 1239 and Y-6b class 2-8-8-2 No. 2197.

All's fair in a battle like this and allegedly there was some mechanical finagling of the 459's engine that, according to EMD's on-site test engineers, allowed each of the four diesel units to churn out 1,700 horsepower, 200 above their normal rating. EMD never officially acknowledged this and the N&W Motive Power Department's Clarence Pond piously refused to discuss any test results when this author approached him on the subject back in 1965.

The tests were conducted on N&W's Scioto and Pocahontas Divisions during the period September 9-27, 1952. The 459 was pitted against the 1239 in the Scioto Division tests and against the 2197 in the Pocahontas Division runs. For test purposes the Pocahontas Division was broken down into two parts: Williamson-to-Farm where the ruling grade was 0.6 percent and Farm-to-Bluefield where the ruling grade was 1.4 percent. Some idea of the relative performance of the two locomotives can be gleaned from the test results shown below:

Williamson-Farm (62 miles)	Load/Time
Y-6b No. 2197	7,481 tons - 2hrs/31 min.
F7ABBA No. 459	7,422 tons - 2hrs/29 min.
Farm-Bluefield (36 miles)	
Y-6b No. 2197	3,818 tons - 1hr/40 min.
F7ABBA No. 459	5,184 tons - 2hrs/2 min.

On the Williamson-Farm segment, with roughly equal loads and running times, the diesel showed a fuel saving per-ton-mile of approximately 6 percent. On the Farm-Bluefield segment, however, fuel costs per-ton-mile were actually less for No. 2197. Where 459 did stand out was in its ability to hoist heavier tonnage up the 1.4 percent grade, thanks to its considerably higher tractive effort at low speeds. In theory, at least, four diesel-powered trains could bring approximately as much tonnage from Farm to Bluefield as five steam-powered ones.

Surely, these results showed that N&W had no option but to substitute diesels for steam on stiff grades, didn't they? Well, no, reasoned N&W management. After all, the steamers *were* paid for and the idea of equipment trusts was still anathema to the pay-as-you-go N&W. Then too, all steam servicing facilities were in place whereas new ones would have to be built to service diesels. Also it would take quite a while to amortize the cost of all those new facilities, let alone the cost of the locomotives they would serve. N&W thanked EMD politely and continued for another three years to power all freight and passenger trains with steam. The 459 ultimately was sold to the Union Pacific.

Was the N&W short-sighted in ignoring the diesel's advantage? Forty years after the fact it is easy to say yes. But which of us back in 1952, blest with a stable full of Superpower steam, spare parts still readily available and the cost of coal competitive with that of oil, would have decided differently?

William E. Warden

Near where the author worked in Waynesboro, Virginia, a Y-6 shakes the ground in 1956 (see below).

For a lineside viewer, a Y was an experience not readily forgotten—all smoke and cinders, blurred side rods cycling up and down 140 times per minute, and banshee wail of a whistle echoing off the nearby Blue Ridge Mountains as it slashed through the quiet of little Luray, Virginia, on an otherwise sleepy June 1954 morning.

Y's seemed to take a sensual joy in tackling grades that A's bore grudgingly as necessary inconveniences. Watch a Y slugging it out with Blue Ridge Grade, her exhaust skyrocketing a hundred feet in the air, and it was hard to consider this piece of machinery incapable of feeling human exultation at besting the mountain. If there were 11,000 tons of coal and steel tied to her tender and a sister Y pushing on the cabin car, so much the better.

You *felt* a Y too, emotionally and physically through the soles of your feet or the seat of your pants, thanks to the physics of dynamic augment created by sixteen 58-inch drivers churning out 45 mph. This author once had the good fortune of working in an office whose windows faced the track, a hundred yards from the Shenandoah Division main. An unvarying sign of an approaching Y was the floor's vibration beneath feet and chair. No sound penetrated this stout brick building but look up and there was a Y and a train passing like some silent ghost. On the Richter scale, a Norfolk & Western 2-8-8-2 at speed was at least a 5.

Y-6/Y-6a/Y-6b Photos

W. E. Warden Coll.

(Above) Official portrait of N&W Y-6b No. 2197, built by Roanoke Shops in 1952 as part of the last group of articulated steam locomotives built in the United States—indeed very nearly the last group of steam locomotives built new in this country. (The Roanoke Shops' S-1a class 0-8-0s of 1953 were the last.) It was the very locomotive that contested against the EMD F7 diesels in the famous tests that same year (see page 27).

H. Reid, W. E. Warden Coll.

(Left) Midst much smoke and steam Y-6 No. 2122 with a westbound freight in tow ducks under a highway bridge at Cambria (near Christiansburg, Virginia) in 1955.

(Below) In September 1958, Y-6 No. 2150 swivels its articulation joint, swinging the boiler away from the front engine as it does a bit of switching behind Blue Ridge Station depot building. The smattering of switching that went on at Blue Ridge due to the presence of Blue Ridge Stone Company (shipping 30 or 40 gondolas of rock per week) was largely overlooked by photographers bent on recording the spectacular fight of big steam against the mighty mountain.

William E. Warden

Bruce Fales, T. W. Dixon Coll.

(Above) Y-6 No. 2126 in a clean portrait view at Hagerstown, Maryland yard in 1935. ***(Left)*** Exhaust exiting the stack at more than 100 miles per hour creates the vast plume of steam, smoke, and cinders—ample evidence that Y-6a No. 2160 is applying all its 5,000-plus horsepower to the cabin car of another eastbound freight at Blue Ridge in September 1958. ***(Below)*** Alas, the late Johnny Krause was famed for not captioning his negatives, so don't know where this photo was taken, showing a mixed freight powered by Y-6a No. 2152.

William E. Warden

John Krause, Ed Crist Coll.

(Right) Y-6b No. 2173 is working hard on the grade near Singer, Virginia, with an eastbound extra. The head brakeman appears to have little to do but gawk at the lensman. Note this this is one of the few N&W official company photos that suggests that the railway's locomotives ever operated other than clear-stacked.

N&W photo, W. R. Baumgardner, Jr. Coll.

(Below) Side and main rods have already been removed from Y-6b No. 2177 at left, a sure indication that the eleven-year-old locomotive's next destination is scrap. But Y-6 No. 2138, ten years its senior, still has steam up in the servicing dock at Williamson, West Virginia, evidence that the older engine will continue to haul freight, but not for long as the date is October 1959, definitely the twilight of N&W steam. Our best guess on why the 2177 was headed for scrapyard while older 2138 was still running is that the flue time had expired and it was cheaper to retire it than to repair it.

William E. Warden

(Below) Although not favored by train watchers as the more famous Blue Ridge Grade, Christiansburg Hill could be just as daunting to a freight train unless a helper was picked up at the bottom of the eastbound grade. Here Y-6 No. 2142 is assisting an eastbound manifest up the Hill just east of Christiansburg station in the summer of 1954. We are past the summit here and No. 2142 is just going along for the ride now and will soon be cut off.

John Krause, T. W. Dixon Coll.

A. L. Julian, Ed Crist Coll.

Y-6b 2174 steams it up on the Dry Fork Branch's high bridge to the delight of the July 1959 "Rail Museum Safari" passengers in the cars behind. The author was aboard the train at the time, so never did get to appreciate the immensity of this bridge.

(Below) You're right; the light load coupled to Y-6 No. 2142 in this September 1958 photo does not justify all that billowing smoke the Mallet is emitting. The lifted pop valves are more in keeping with the tonnage of this Roanoke-Lynchburg local aproaching Blue Ridge. What did account for the pyrotechnics was some wheeling and dealing between the photographer's companion and the engine crew back at the Webster Brick siding.

William E. Warden

Y-6a No. 2156 sits alone at Lynchburg Union Station September 6, 1958.

Y-6 No. 2123 with auxiliary tender works hard upgrade with a nice display of heavy exhaust in this September 9, 1958 view. Location is not known.

(all) Bob's Photo

In Roanoke on June 1, 1956, Y-6b No. 2176 moves an eastbound freight through the yard. At the right are several passenger cars adjacent to the station platform and shed.

Jeff Sanders Coll.

Ed King

(Above) Y-6b No. 2173 is moving freight cars around the yard in this cold sunny scene. The angle of the photo accentuates the girth of the locomotive's ample boiler, and quite well illustrates the piping from the forward low-pressure cylinders into the smokebox area.

(Left) Y-6 No. 2145 and a brother locomotive rest near the coaling station at Iaeger, West Virginia, in July 1959, in the twilight of steam on the N&W.

Eugene L. Huddleston

(Right) Old Y-3a No. 2051 (ALCO-Richmond, 1923) rests from switcher duties at the Portsmouth, Ohio engine terminal in October 1958. A Y-6's auxiliary tender is backed up to the 2051's tender, and in the right background stands a J-class 4-8-4.

White steam exhaust issues from Y-6a No. 2166 as it runs light in shifter duty at Kermit, West Virginia, in January 1959. The rusty boiler front tells us that this locomotive is in its last phase of service.

Y-6 No. 2138, the "second pigeon" (second shift) mine shifter goes about its coal hopper shuffling duties at the Island Creek Coal Company's tipple near Delbarton, West Virginia, in December 1958.

(all) Eugene L. Huddleston

This very clear overhead photo of Y-3 No. 2037 on the Portsmouth yard in 1958 shows the top of the tender, including the head breakman's "doghouse," to good advantage. Overfire jets hanging on the side of the smokebox are also clearly evident in this photo.

(Left) Y-6 No. 2137 and a coal train pose for the company photographer at Spout Springs, Virginia, about 17 miles east of Lynchburg, in August 1939, en route to the dumpers at Lambert's Point in Norfolk. Considering a company photographer could pretty well dictate where he wanted a train posed, we wonder why this one didn't spot 2137 and its train in a position that would have allowed him to photograph the sunny side of the train.

N&W photo, W. E. Warden Coll.

(Below, left) Y-6a No. 2157 thunders past block signal while accelerating an eastbound coal drag toward Blue Ridge grade. The exhaust from the helper, more than a mile distant, is visible at left. Near Bonsack, Virginia, in the early 1950s. ***(Below, right)*** A clean 2135 works a freight up Blue Ridge grade in June 1954.

N&W Photo, Robert D. Simpson Coll.

John Krause, T. W. Dixon Coll.

Y-6 No. 2125 with a hot shot freight in tow emerges from Montgomery Tunnel, near Christiansburg, Virginia, in July 1955.

Ed Crist Coll.

Y-6b No. 2187 is eastbound, passing through Christiansburg, on a winter morning in 1954. The brick passenger station is in the left background. There was nothing like cool weather to create spectacular steam locomotive performances.

John Krause, T. W. Dixon Coll.

Clear stacked, Y-6b No. 2183 rolls around a curve east of Bluefield with yet another train of mine-bound empty hopper cars, part of the never-ending back-and-forth between mine and market.

H. Reid

John Krause, W. E. Warden Coll.

Y-6a No. 2163 is headed for Roanoke with a westbound train of empties as an eastbound approaches in the foreground. In the background to the right is another 2-8-8-2 that will assist the eastbound up Blue Ridge grade. The scene is near Vinton, Virginia, a suburb of Roanoke.

N&W RY.
CARRIER OF
FUEL SATISFACTION

(Below) Y-6b No. 2170 sits at the Bluefield engine terminal with No. 2160 and at least three other Y-6s, including several under the smoke-abatement devices in the background in July 1956. Y-3 No. 2040, brakemen riding the footboards, goes about its duties as a switcher in the foreground. The N&W YMCA is the prominent structure across the street. YMCAs were an important part of the railroad scene until comparatively recent times.

Joe Schmitz

(both) William E. Warden

Nudged against the caboose of an eastbound manifest at Bonsack, Virginia, in September 1958, No. 2160 is cranked up to nearly 50 mph, but ahead is 7,000 tons of freight led by an A-class 2-6-6-4 and the tortuous Blue Ridge climb.

Southbound extra Y-6b 2175 slashes through the quiet Shenandoah Valley town of Luray on a peaceful June 1954 morning. The station at left once served thousands of passengers who came here to visit the famous Luray Caverns.

Jim Shaughnessy

On a fine August day in 1958, Y-6a No. 2167 leads an A-class 2-6-6-4 up Blue Ridge. Within six months diesels would conquer this run. The whining of traction motors and clatter of internal combustion engines are poor substitutes for the symphony of shotgun exhausts that one can almost hear in this scene.

Jim Shaw

Larry Fellure, Ed Crist Coll.

(Above) Y-6 No. 2136 and a string of empty hoppers are West Virginia-bound, ducking under US 460 near Ripplemead, Virginia, in April 1956. Spring is late in coming to the Allegheny Mountains and the trees are still nude of foliage. This photo particularly accentuates the Y-6's giant pilot deck, with its headlight atop the two steam exhaust pipes from the low-pressure cylinders, and the crossed hand-rails in front. If ever there was a Mallet that lived up to its inventor's dream, it was the N&W's modern Y's.

(Left) This scene is in the roundhouse at Williamson, West Virginia, in the very final days of steam. It appears that Y-6 No. 2123 is being given some minor repairs. And the scene could easily and without challenge be labeled 1955—or 1945 for that matter. However, the last steam locomotive ran for the last time just 15 days after this photograph was actually taken on April 21, 1960.

(Right) With its coal bunker topped off, Y-6 No. 2152 and its boiler shiny black appears to be waiting for another load of coal from West Virginia to tote westward from Portsmouth, Ohio, in April 1956. The coal's destination? Columbus probably, an interchange with the New York Central or Pennsylvania, and then Ohio, Indiana, Illinois, or Michigan steel mills and power plants.

(Below) Y-6b No. 2194 is on point of manifest freight No. 84 at Switchback, West Virginia, in 1958 in an impressive action photo.

Jim Shaw

Benjamin S. Stopper. W. E. Warden Coll.

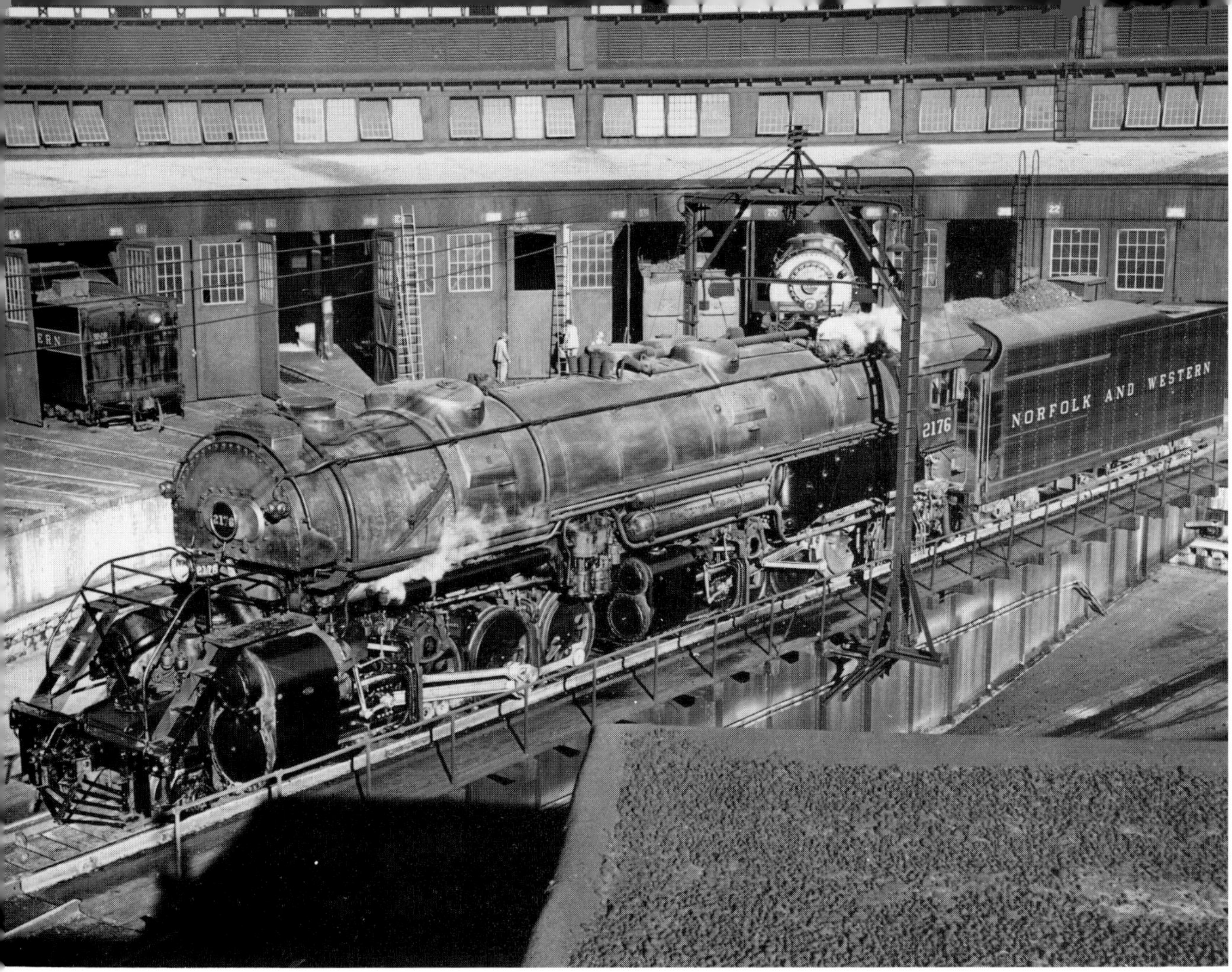

N&W photo, W. R. Baumgardner, Jr. Coll.

Almost fresh out of Roanoke Shops, Y-6b No. 2176 poses on the Shaffers Crossing turntable in December 1948. The 2176 is en route to rest in one of the roundhouse stalls between assignments.

Bad luck! Y-6a No. 2170 is coming up to the aid of a stalled coal train at Christiansburg, Virginia, June 6, 1954.

C. W. Jernstrom, Ed Crist Coll.

Philip R. Hastings, Ed Crist Coll.

(Right) Hagerstown yard's skyline was dominated by this huge concrete coaling tower shared by the Pennsylvania Railroad and N&W. Right now Y-6b No. 2173 is making use of the tower's coal bunker. Taken about 1953.

(Below) S-1a class 0-8-0 No. 266 (left) shares Shenandoah Yard with Y-6 No. 2152 (right) on an October Sunday afternoon in 1956. The 2152 has just pulled into the yard with a Hagerstown-bound manifest freight. The Shenandoah passenger station, then still visited by New York-Roanoke Train Nos. 1 and 2, is at the left. The switcher, imported from neighboring Chesapeake & Ohio in 1950, is a 1948 Baldwin Locomotive Works product, and shares chores at this important division point with an M-2 class 4-8-0.

William E. Warden

William E. Warden

Overcast skies and intermittent rain plagued the October 1959 "Rail Museum Safari" excursion train, but at Williamson the sun came out long enough to shine on (left to right) Y-6b No. 2175, Y-6 No. 2123, and S-1a class 0-8-0 No. 225, all scrubbed and polished for the excursionists. Alas, for all their brave appearance, the three locomotives would be taken out of service permanently before another year had passed.

The exhaust of Y-6b No. 2193 is echoing off the rocks near Bluefield in July 1955. Why the locomotive doesn't have an auxiliary water tender at this late date we don't know. Perhaps it's a relatively short train and no "canteen" was needed.

Ed Crist Coll.

N&W photo, Ed Crist Coll.

(Above) Y-6b No. 2181 takes a freight across the high bridge at remote Cedar Bluff, Virginia, in the early 1950s, flying prominent white flags. ***(Below)*** Proof that A-class 2-6-6-4s didn't get all the starring roles, a Y-6b (No. 2173) and Y-6 (No. 2129) speed a freight east in August 1958 near the foot of Blue Ridge grade, accelerating here to near their top speed, but at the top of the grade they'll be down to about 10 mph.

Jim Shaughnessy

William E. Warden

Amid a blizzard of smoke and cinders, Y-6 No. 2142 gets underway at Blue Ridge with an eastbound local in September 1958. The Mallet had been in the siding while *The Tenneesean* cleared the main. Surely this was steam railroading at its best for the trackside watcher and, we suspect, for the 2142's crew also.

N&W photo, Ed Crist Coll.

(Above) Y-6b No. 2181 takes a freight across the high bridge at remote Cedar Bluff, Virginia, in the early 1950s, flying prominent white flags. ***(Below)*** Proof that A-class 2-6-6-4s didn't get all the starring roles, a Y-6b (No. 2173) and Y-6 (No. 2129) speed a freight east in August 1958 near the foot of Blue Ridge grade, accelerating here to near their top speed, but at the top of the grade they'll be down to about 10 mph.

Jim Shaughnessy

William E. Warden

Amid a blizzard of smoke and cinders, Y-6 No. 2142 gets underway at Blue Ridge with an eastbound local in September 1958. The Mallet had been in the siding while *The Tenneesean* cleared the main. Surely this was steam railroading at its best for the trackside watcher and, we suspect, for the 2142's crew also.

(both) L. W. Rice, T. W. Dixon Coll.

(Above and right) Y-6 No. 2152 poses at Shenandoah, Virginia, front and rear on September 5, 1954. That streamlined locomotive in the distance in the top photo isn't a J, but a streamlined K-2 or K-2a Mountain type that often handled passenger and mixed trains on the Shenandoah Division.

N&W photo, W. R. Baumgardner Coll.

Y-6a No. 2165 demonstrates what happens when the fill under the track structure is washed away by heavy rain. This hapless Mallet is in Bluefield yard in June 1954.

N&W photo, W. E. Baumgardner Coll.

Richard J. Cook, Sr.

(Above) Y-6a No. 2167 with a westbound extra sweeps around another bend in New River, this one at Pearisburg, Virginia, in 1952. The Pearisburg station nestles just under the bridge in the background that carries US Route 460 across the railroad and the river. One of the joys of being a company photographer must have been the ability to schedule your shoot on a day with perfect weather and to have trains posed as needed.

(Left) Y-6a No. 2161 and 41 cars of mixed freight roll northward on the Shenandoah Division near Lithia, Virginia, at 8:53 a.m. on April 11, 1951.

(Above) Engineer of a Y-6 was king of all he surveyed. In 1955, the hogger-king of No. 2145 looks down on a small portion of his kingdom at Shenandoah Junction from a vantage point of fourteen feet up. "Hogger" was railroad slang for engineer, taken from the nickname of big slow steam locomotives, called "hogs."

(Above) Y-6 No. 2145 is assaulting the grade at Lyndhurst on the Shenandoah Division with a mile-long manifest freight in January 1957. This drama would not be replayed very many more times as the whole Shenandoah Division was dieselized less than three weeks later. The Blue Ridge Mountains are in the right background. The light-colored streak at the base of the mountain is a gravel pit created in the 1850s when Claudius Crozet, Virginia's great pioneer civil engineer, cut through and tunneled under these mountains near Waynesboro to create the Blue Ridge Railroad. This road was soon absorbed into what was later the Chesapeake & Ohio (whose Mountain Subdivision crossed the N&W's Shenandoah line at Waynesboro).

(all)William E. Warden

(Right) The rear brakeman and conductor of the southbound manifest at left are out looking for dragging brake riggings and other defects on the northbound freight behind Y-6 No. 2132. The northbound train is in the hole at Waynesboro, Virginia, but should get a clear board at any moment to head for Shenandoah. It is about 7:00 a.m. on a cool April morning in 1956.

Just another Y pushing a coal drag? Not exactly. Y-6 No. 2125 is leaning into a train at Natural Bridge Station on the Shenandoah Division, where helpers were seldom required. There were occasions, however, when the grades around Natural Bridge, Pkin, and Lofton would tax the capability of a single Y on the head end and a helper would be needed. This was a frequent occurrance during the heavy traffic of World War II. Y-6s were rated at 3,000 tons, but during the war 6,000-ton trains were the norm, with a second Y-6 pushing from Roanoke to Lofton. However, in the summer of 1954, when this photo was taken, it was an exception.

John Krause, T. W. Dixon Coll.

All smoke, steam and business, Y-6 No. 2134 at right muscles another eastbound freight up Blue Ridge grade, while on the left Z-1b class 2-6-6-2, perhaps dreaming of the days when she performed such important jobs as this helper, waits patiently with a humble work train.

Richard J. Cook, Sr.

William E. Warden

Y-6a No. 2156 rests beneath the coaling station at Williamson, West Virginia, on June 18, 1949. Williamson was an important terminal, not only for through trains, but as the center for numerous coal branches serving scores of mines in the West Virginia Pocahontas coal fields. It had large modern engine servicing facilities.

Block signals bracket eastbound extra just east of Singer, Virginia, about 1950. Y-6b No. 2173 is spewing out a clean white exhaust, pulling a train of box cars, refrigerators, and other mixed freight.

N&W photo, Robert D. Simpson Coll.

On the Radford-Bristol line in the summer of 1954 Y-6b No. 2177 snakes a mixed freight train through this hilly country.

John Krause, T. W. Dixon Coll.

William E. Warden

With 6,000 horsepower of superheated steam behind him and about 7,000 tons of manifest freight in front in July 1958, perhaps standing on the deck of the cabin car *is* the most prudent thing for the rear brakeman to do here on Blue Ridge grade. If one of those two opposing forces overcomes the other it will be time to hit the cinders! But cabooses rarely crumpled on this grade and the brakeman is simply enjoying the summer weather and keeping an eye out for hot boxes.

(Left) Y-6a No. 2163 smokes past the attractive depot at Farmville, Virginia, en route to Roanoke and points west. This station and a make-believe N&W passenger train were used in a popular TV commercial of the mid 1980s.

John Krause, T. W. Dixon Coll.

(Below) Running extra, Y-6a No. 2151 and its train of eastbound coal hug the bank of New River in 1941. Arch bridge in background carries US Route 460 across the river. Both bridge and highway have since been relocated.

N&W photo, W. R. Baumgardner Coll.

C. W. Jernstrom, W. E. Warden Coll.

A meet takes place on Christiansburg Hill between J-class 4-8-4 No. 600 (left), the first J, and Y-6 No. 2140 on a cold December 1954 day. Note the passing track, long since removed, between the two main lines.

Against a Blue Ridge Mountain background in 1956, 4-8-2 (K-2 class) No. 122 meets Y-6b No. 2200 atop US Route 460 underpass near Villamont, Virginia. The 4-8-2 has the Roanoke-Norfolk local passenger train in tow, and the Mallet's load could be anything from fast freight to empty hoppers. US 460 is now four lanes here and in 1992 the old underpass was removed and the N&W mainline realigned about 100 feet to the north on a new bridge.

John Krause, W. E. Warden Coll.

William E. Warden

A northbound freight behind Y-6 No. 2143 ducks under a highway overpass at Waynesboro, Virginia, en route to Hagerstown, at the northern end of the Shenandoah Division, in June 1956. The Shenandoah Division was a very important route during WWII, bypassing the congestions at Potomac Yard near Washington. In 1939 it generated 91,213,000 gross ton-miles, contrasted with 558,557,000 in 1943! CTC and 10.5 miles of new double track installed in 1943 helped speed the traffic.

The summer of 1954 found Y-6a No. 2163 pounding across a fill near the eastern base of Blue Ridge with a string of empties. Like its neighboring competitor C&O, N&W's hoppers were usually equipped with end extensions so that coal could be heaped.

John Krause, T. W. Dixon Coll.

The condensate escaping from the various portions of Y-6b No. 2182 attests to the fact that it is a cold day in April 1956, on Bluefield yard. Note the array of handrails on the front of the locomotive, including the crossed set on the pilot deck and the one around the top of the smokebox.

Jim Shaw

Y-6b No. 2179 is huffing into Bluefield with a westbound extra time freight in August 1954. This was during the period when the Y's intended for through freights acquired their auxiliary water tenders. It can't be determined if No. 2179 was one of the first or last to be so equipped.

W. R. Baumgardner, Jr. Coll.

(Right) Y-6b No. 2173 roars out of the tunnel at Pembroke, Virginia, on an eastbound manifest freight on June 14, 1956. Both the works of nature and of man are impressive in this photo. Note slide fencing to the left.

(Below) On the approach to the overpass crossing the B&O main line at Shenandoah Junction, West Virginia, Y-6b No. 2173 with a local from Hagerstown cants into a curve in June 1958. No. 2173 will spend about an hour shunting cars at the junction, picking up some and setting out others for the B&O, then head for Charles Town, Berryville, White Post, Front Royal, Luray, and finally Shenandoah.

Richard J. Cook, Sr.

William E. Warden

Jim Shaughnessy

Y-6b No. 2173 leads Y-6 No. 2129 east of Blue Ridge on an eastbound train. Nothing disturbs the indifferent cows in this pastoral scene, but after all this occured at least two dozen times daily.

J. R. Quinn

In another bucolic scene with the Blue Ridge as a backdrop, Y-6 No. 2139 races across the floor of the fertile Shenandoah Valley northbound near Shenandoah in late October 1955. "Shenandoah" is an Algonquin name, loosely translated meaning "Daughter of the Stars."

William E. Warden, Bart Gregg Coll.

Y-6 No. 2142 has just spent the better part of an hour switching cars around Blue Ridge and is now wasting no time getting out of town with its Roanoke-Lynchburg local freight in September 1958. The white tipple in the background with hoppers under it isn't for coal, but stone, from a nearby quarry.

Robert D. Simpson Coll.

Again near the crest of Blue Ridge grade, a Y-6a and an A-class 2-6-6-4 struggle mightily toward the summit. The white patina on the left (eastbound) rails and roadbed is the sand laid down by a thousand steamers struggling to keep their footing on this daunting grade. Probably taken about 1950.

John Krause, T. W. Dixon Coll.

(Above) Y-6b No. 2173 runs light in reverse in a passing siding near Blue Ridge in the winter of 1954. The locomotive had probably just finished helper work and is returning to base.

(Left) Y-6b No. 2186 pounds through Elliston, Virginia, in April 1956 with a mile-long fast freight in tow. Life for the powerful Mallets wasn't all coal drags in the mountains, but also were preferred on fast freights on the Bluefield-Roanoke run. The A-class 2-6-6-4s could run like the wind with almost any weight train on level territory, but in these steep hills the Y's had the gross ton-mile-per-hour edge.

William E. Warden

Jim Shaw

(Right) Y-6b No. 2173 and its obliging crew take a moment out from switching chores at Shenandoah Junction to pose for the photographer. Earlier, the 2173 had steamed into town with a local freight from Hagerstown.

Two Y-6s, 2150 at left and 2141 at right, face off at Waynesboro, Virginia, on a cool spring morning in 1956. Although the Mallets appear to be running on wrong track, No. 2150 is actually in a siding and will head north as soon as 2141 clears. This photo illustrates quite well how the Y's firebox was hung over its rear set of driving wheels rather than being supported largely by a trailing truck as with the A's and many other big articulateds.

(Left) The essence of modern steam power: 39-inch-diameter low-pressure cylinders, roller bearings on the pilot truck, and a boiler so fat that the stack barely extends above it. All these show clearly in this profile of Y-6b No. 2150's front end at the peak of the Blue Ridge grade in July 1958.

(all) William E. Warden

(Right) The October 1957 day was raw and gusty, a not uncommon occurence in the Blue Ridge at that time just preceding Indian Summer. And although the photographer was bone-cold, it was just another day for Y-6 No. 2145 as it comes slogging up the grade at the rear of still another coal drag. Business was hefty enough on that particular Saturday to keep two 2-8-8-2s in pusher service.

N&W photo, W. E. Warden Coll.

In a job that must have been the envy of every train watcher in history, an unidentified company photographer prepares a ponderous 8x10 view camera to capture an image of newly-built Y-6b No. 2171 in 1948.

William E. Warden

In September 1958, the crew of Y-6a No. 2160 mug cheerfully for the photographer's Crown Graphic 4x5 press camera. The 2160 is on the Boaz pusher siding east of Vinton and there's not much for the crew to do except gab with visiting train watchers until the next freight arrived for a push up Blue Ridge grade. The job of a helper crew was not the most exciting one on the railroad except for those thirty minutes a dozen times a day when help was needed in boosting tonnage over the grade. Then, as the pusher gradually shouldered more of the load, everything was all business plus the drama of shotgun exhausts, cinder blizzards, and the thrill and pride that went with one of the most important jobs on the Norfolk Division. Incidentally, you'll not find Boaz on any road map or in any timetable; the siding was there and nothing more.